Walking with a Stranger c[...]
in its own right, or as the first in a series of four, titled *Soul Survivor Life*.

The aim of the series is to explain the basics of Christianity and Christian living in down-to-earth, jargon-free language. The four books follow the pattern of life: birth, adolescence, mid-life crisis and death. The first, *Walking with a Stranger*, explores what it really means to become a Christian, who God is and how we can build a personal relationship with him. *My First Trousers* looks at the challenges and rewards facing us when we start going deeper with Jesus. The Christian life is not easy, however, and *Weeping Before an Empty Tomb* asks how we cope when the going gets tough. The final book, *Afterlife*, is about facing the future, in particular death, heaven and eternity.

Mike Pilavachi is the founder of Soul Survivor and pastor of Soul Survivor, Watford. Craig Borlase is a free-lance writer. They have previously written two other books together, *Live the Life* and *For the Audience of One* (both Hodder Christian Books).

can be read either as a single book

Walking with a Stranger

Discovering God

Mike Pilavachi with Craig Borlase

Hodder & Stoughton
LONDON SYDNEY AUCKLAND

British Library Cataloguing in Publication Data
A record for this book is available from the British Library

ISBN 0 340 73534 1

Typeset by Avon Dataset Ltd, Bidford-on-Avon, Warks

Printed and bound in Great Britain by
Clays Ltd, St Ives plc

Hodder & Stoughton
A Division of Hodder Headline
338 Euston Road
London NW1 3BH

To Rob, Sue, Paul and Mick Taylor,
my South African family.

Contents

Acknowledgements

Thanks to all those who have paid the price for the writing of this book, particularly my friends and colleagues at Soul Survivor and the church family at Soul Survivor Watford. Special thanks go to Andrew Latimer and Andy Baldwin, two wonderful servants of God who have been such an encouragement to me, and to Chris and Belinda Russell, who came to the rescue in my hour of need. As in the past, I'd also like to express my appreciation to Matt and Beth Redman, who suffered with me in the writing of this book, as they seem to do with everything I'm involved in.

1

Is There a God?

If you're reading this book the chances are that you're vaguely interested in this question. Of course there's always a chance that you're reading this book because you've somehow got stuck in a cottage in a remote part of Scotland where the weather is terrible and the only choice of reading material is between this, the back of the bleach bottle and a pre-war textbook on urban waste disposal. If that's the case, then thanks for giving us a go and I hope you find it as exciting as the bleach bottle.

Getting back to the first lot of readers, I might be wrong, but I suppose that you might be open-minded about the existence of God. It may be that there have been times when you have sensed that there's something more behind and beyond the material world. You might have been looking at a beautiful sunset and wondered whether something so beautiful could really have come about by chance. If the world is a painting, then maybe you're wondering if there is an artist.

There might be other reasons why you're thinking about God. You may have been in love and wondered whether there is a personal God who makes sense of our ability to love and feel deeply for one another. You might have wondered about love, loyalty and commitment: could they really come about by chance? Then again, you might not be into art or love. You might have come at it from a more scientific angle, wondering as you studied the laws of nature whether there could be a creator who set them up in the first place. If you're looking for an answer to 'Is there a God?', then this book is written for you. I'll tell you what I believe and know, but don't take my word for it, why not ask him yourself?

Until I was fifteen I called myself an atheist. I even wrote an essay in my English class titled 'Why I am not a Christian'. To my mind Christianity was for old people who were scared of dying, for ignorant people who did not realise that Science had the answers and for weak people who needed a crutch. On paper I was steaming: throwing in argument after argument that I thought exposed Christianity as a fake. The trouble was that even while I was writing I had a sense that there must be more. I had a gut feeling that there must be an intelligent power which could make sense of the order and beauty of the universe. Somewhere, I wanted to believe in a power that would explain the sense of purpose that I felt in my own life. Even though I wrote the opposite, I couldn't accept that my existence was the result of a purposeless accident and nothing more.

Then I became friends with two brothers at school. They had 'something about them', something that was so hard to define but that was easy to like. I'm not talking about popularity here or being able to tell good gags; what the Patkai boys had was something extra. They seemed happy and secure, they were interested in people and they didn't have to put people down to feel good themselves. Whenever I spent time with them I felt better about myself.

I decided that I wanted whatever it was that they had. Then I found out they were Christians. I must have forgotten about my future career as a famous atheist because this didn't really bother me that much. They were the first Christians I had stumbled across and they weren't half as bad as I had expected. They knew how to enjoy themselves, they were normal and popular. Their own sense of assurance was something I longed for, and through them I found out that Christianity is not a set of rules and ceremonies, but something far more exciting: a relationship. I found out the truth about what I had always suspected deep inside:

that there is a God who created us for a reason. We can get to know him ourselves because he wants to have a relationship with his creatures – but not just as pets: God wants that relationship to be just like a relationship between a Father and his children.

In this book I want to try and show you some of my own discoveries about God. Because you might not believe me I've also asked a few of my friends to help me. They're going to tell their stories and all I ask is that you be open-minded and open-hearted about what we say.

If you're reading this book in the rainy Scottish cottage, you've probably already asked yourself why it is that Christians spend so much time trying to convert people. Wouldn't it all be so much nicer if people like me shut up and kept our beliefs to ourselves, leaving people like you to go about your own life in peace? Undoubtedly there have been times when we Christians have been so keen to tell people about what we believe that we've treated people less like humans and more like grapes; there to be picked, crushed and forced into something that they were not before. Instead of it being the good news of Jesus, we've left people with a bitter aftertaste that has reminded them of every reason why they are not a Christian. Sometimes we have given the impression that we have the monopoly on the truth, that we have no intention of listening to what anyone else has to say.

For all of these things I'm sorry. But I can't be sorry for the fact that we're keen. After all, if you had made a discovery which changed your life and brought you great joy, and you knew that this discovery would do the same for others, wouldn't you want them to know about it?

I'm a fan of a guy called C.S. Lewis. He was a clever bloke whom you've probably heard of as the author of the *Chronicles of Narnia*, especially the second book called *The Lion, the Witch and the Wardrobe*. One of his other books was called *Surprised by Joy*, and in it he describes the times in his early life when he caught glimpses of something beyond the material world. These times when he sensed that there is something more to life than death were unusual, and became the start of his change from being an atheist to a Christian. He called these times *moments of joy* and I'm assuming that they must have been surprising.

Even though he didn't know it at the time, he was actually meeting with God. It took years for him to suss this out, but in time God drew back a curtain to show himself as the source of those moments of joy. When Lewis found God (or should I say when God found him) things fell into place.

After Jesus died on the cross his disciples were totally distressed; their leader had been taken from them and they couldn't decide what to do next.

Should they lay low and avoid further persecution at the hands of the Romans, or should they carry on where their master had left off? One day two of them were walking to a village called Emmaus, which was about seven miles from Jerusalem. The Bible continues the story:

They were talking with each other about everything that had happened. As they talked and discussed these things with each other, Jesus himself came up and walked along with them; but they were kept from recognising him.

He asked them, 'What are you discussing together as you walk along?'

They stood still, their faces downcast. One of them, named Cleopas, asked him, 'Are you only a visitor to Jerusalem and do not know the things that have happened there in these days?'

'What things?' he asked.

'About Jesus of Nazareth,' they replied. 'He was a prophet, powerful in word and deed before God and all the people. The chief priests and our rulers handed him over to be sentenced to death, and they crucified him; but we had hoped that he was the one who was going to redeem Israel. And what is more, it is the third day since all this took place. In addition, some of our women amazed us. They went to the tomb early this morning but didn't find his body. They came and told us they had seen

6

a vision of angels, who said he was alive. Then some of our companions went to the tomb and found it just as the women had said, but him they did not see.'

He said to them, 'How foolish you are, and how slow of heart to believe all that the prophets have spoken! Did not the Christ have to suffer these things and then enter his glory?' And beginning with Moses and all the Prophets, he explained to them what was said in all the Scriptures concerning himself.

As they approached the village to which they were going, Jesus acted as if he were going further. But they urged him strongly, 'Stay with us, for it is nearly evening; the day is almost over.' So he went in to stay with them.

When he was at the table with them, he took bread, gave thanks, broke it and began to give it to them. Then their eyes were opened and they recognised him, and he disappeared from their sight. They asked each other, 'Were not our hearts burning within us while he talked with us on the road and opened the Scriptures to us?' (Luke 24: 13–32)

These two disciples thought they were walking with a stranger. They were so dosed up on their own pain and assumptions about life, death and the universe that they failed to recognise God walking alongside them. It was only when Jesus revealed himself to them through what he said and what he did that the penny dropped. I love their response: 'Were not our hearts burning within us?' It's one of the classic understatements in the Bible. Just think about it: if you saw someone rise from the dead, having a slightly increased heartbeat would be the least dramatic of your symptoms.

This has been the experience of millions of men and women down the centuries. It was C.S. Lewis's experience. It is my experience. It's the experience of my friends. I thought I was walking through life with a stranger – a world that only half made sense. At some points along the way my heart burned within me as I sensed something out of the ordinary, but I could never put my finger on what it was. Then one day he revealed himself to me.

I've already told you that I want to talk about some of the things I've discovered about God. I suppose, on reflection, it would be more accurate to say that he discovered me. He made himself visible to me. The glimpses of joy, the sense of the heart burning, the desire to see something beyond the material world, all this made sense when I discovered Jesus and Jesus discovered me. I know this is a bit of a cliché, but the lights in my head came on. When I met Jesus I knew that I had come home. It is my hope and prayer that, as you read this book, you will be surprised by joy, that you will recognise the stranger and that you will come to know him as a friend.

2

God is Personal

If I'm right about this whole God thing – if he does exist and is more than just a collection of strange gases or an old bloke with a beard – then doesn't it make sense that he would give us clues about how to find him? I mean, if he is interested in our lives, if he does want to walk alongside us just as Jesus did with the chaps on the way to Emmaus, then it would be kind of stupid if he did all that he could to avoid us. Avoiding people is the sort of thing we do – especially when it comes down to gimpy weirdos who want to tell us about how to farm cockroaches; it is not the kind of thing that God does.

I'm convinced that God speaks to his people. Just like the rest of us, he is into communication. OK, so we may be a little short on booming voices and giant fingers pointing down from the sky, but just take a look around you and you will see the marks of God's communications. Open your eyes and you'll see his mail all over the place: in nature, other people, events and most immediately through the Bible. That book didn't just float down from heaven one day, pre-packed, sealed and written on tablets of stone or chunks of wood. The Bible is a history told by many different writers spanning well over two thousand years. It is the ultimate story book, and is stuffed full of tales and sagas, each of which adds a new detail to the greater picture that we see forming throughout. The Bible is history; it is *his* story. We're not talking about some pasty-faced pop star here, but the Creator of heaven and earth: God.

Some of those classic stories that we find on the pages of the Bible tell us about people like Abraham, Isaac, Jacob; three ancient guys whom God blessed and made the fathers of the nation of Israel. There's the tale of Moses: a man who led a nation out of slavery, through the Red Sea and almost into the promised land. There's David, the greatest King of Israel; Solomon, the wise one; and there are even descriptions of the birth of Christianity as the early Church fought oppression and persecution to become established and grow into what it is today. But it's more than that. Mixed in with the stories of these very real characters is the story of God. The Bible is his book: it was written by men, but Christians believe that the people who wrote it were inspired by the Holy Spirit. The result is a true, accurate and fantastic revelation of who God is.

This personal God that we're reading about now decided to inspire the Bible in order that we might have some type of map. It may not tell us which star we need to turn left at to get to heaven, but it does tell us which Son we need to follow to find eternal life. Of course, like any map, just reading it at home is no substitute for taking the journey itself. We need to get on with the job of using the Bible as a tool for understanding God, as a blueprint for how we should live our lives to please him. But if you really are serious about starting out on this journey, having a decent look at the map is a pretty sensible place to start.

Now I don't want you to think that I can't make up my mind, but I've just had another idea. The Bible, as well as being a map, is also a love letter. OK, so it's a pretty long one and has an unusually high proportion of death and famine in it, but it's a love letter nevertheless. Read it and you find out about how God expresses his love for his people through all generations. It clearly shows us all the things that God has done for us, not because he was forced into it, but simply because of his intense love for those he has created.

God is personal and created us to enjoy a relationship with him. In case you hadn't noticed, something's not quite right and we're definitely not living in a free-flowing paradise with God. There's evil around us – wars, oppression and poverty – and the Bible tells us where we went wrong. In giving us free will, God allowed us to make up our own minds, and by doing that he gave us personality. He gave us freedom to make our own choices, even if that meant some of those choices would be mistaken. If he hadn't have done, we would have been no more than robots, responding to his love and expressing devotion simply because we were programmed to. Think about a mother: what would give her more joy – a shop-bought card with tacky message inside given on Mother's Day or a home made one with a simple 'I love you', made not because of a marketing ploy but because the child meant it? Like God, we would all rather have love from a person that chose to love us than from a computer that was programmed.

God gave us the knowledge of how to choose between good and evil; it was up to us which one we decided to follow. I'm not talking about the choice between good and evil being like choosing between eating one sweet or eating ten, but choosing whether or not to live in relationship with him. This is precisely what the story of Adam and Eve is about, but it's also something that's going on in our lives today. Right now you can decide to follow good or evil. It really is that black and white. Do we choose to have a relationship with God or do we choose to ignore him? How can I say this? Because life is not about money, power or sex. At the end of it all we were created for one thing – to have relationship with God.

Things do get a little more complicated than this though. After all, if it was a straight choice between God and no God without any consequences or responsibilities then there wouldn't be so much to get quite so worked up about. The truth is that things get messy because of sin. We can define sin as going away from God; as someone old once said, sin is not first of all badness, but awayness. We'll look at it in detail in the next chapter, but Jesus tells a wonderful story about a son who wanders off away from his father. When he goes walkabout he gets involved in some bad things, but the problems didn't all begin when he got high and slept with prostitutes. They started when he decided to part ways with his dad. He broke the natural law of relationship, wishing that his father was dead and putting an end to their relationship. That's exactly what sin is: going away from our Father in heaven; choosing to do our own thing instead of keeping close to him. The son's choice is still on offer to us today: will we live a life of arrogant independence from God or a life of connection with him as our Father?

The Bible tells the story of how the human race decided to turn away from God, to go it alone, and from that moment on the Bible is a heart-wrenching story of God's efforts to woo and win back the human race. It always amazes me when I look at the Bible, no matter how many times I've thought about it, but from every page the message screams that God hasn't given up on us yet. We've turned our back on our Creator – the One who gave us life; we've destroyed one another; we've raped one another; we've oppressed the weak and have chained up the poor. We're not talking about ancient history here, but about places that are just a short flight away from Heathrow; at the end of the twentieth century we're still counting the dead in Bosnia, Kosovo and Rwanda. All of these tragedies have come as a consequence of our decision to turn away from God.

What has he done through all this? He has stayed with us. Just like we read in the Bible, God today is still full of mercy and forgiveness, still prepared for us to make up our minds to follow him, stumbling along the way. He is full of character and emotions and feelings, and the Bible isn't afraid to show it. At times we read about how he is a joyful God, one who gets jealous over his people – not in a possessive way but because he yearns for them to come back to him. We see how he gets angry when he witnesses injustice, sin, hatred and evil. The Bible tells us how he loves us too. It describes him as being like a mother hen, brooding over us by being tender and compassionate. Ultimately the revelation that we see of God is that he became a human being, that the Creator became like his creation so that we might find our way home.

Most of us today are suspicious of institutions.

We've seen the failure of the giants that our grand-parents used to trust, and have grown up to be wary and suspicious of people who claim to be right. It started with Watergate: suddenly governments were not squeaky clean, corruption was not beneath them and the most powerful man in the world was unveiled as a cheat and a liar. The assassination of JFK and the death of Marilyn Monroe suggested that those who held the real political power might also have blood on their hands. The truth about Communism was revealed and the Berlin Wall came down – behind it wasn't the proud honesty of a political system that claimed to be 'for the people', but a lot of poor and oppressed people who wanted out. Then they tried to set Capitalism free in Russia, hoping that it would show the whole world that it was the best way forward. What happened? Corruption and greed took over and left the people in an even worse state than when they started. 'Yes, things were bad under Communism,' they said in Moscow, 'but at least we knew where we stood.' The politicians lined their own pockets and the President stocked up his drinks cabinet. In the first ten years that Russia spent out of Communism, the life expectancy of the average man in Moscow reduced from 66 to 56. So much for the great white hope.

Back in America the CIA was linked to killings of anyone from John Lennon (for being 'dangerous') to Martin Luther King (for being right). It has been alleged that they started wars to save political butts and set up dictators that they could control. In the UK three of our Queen's children's marriages have ended up in tatters while prominent politicians were found dead in bondage gear, or receiving back-handers from foreign businessmen or living lies on the greatest of scales.

We've seen the rise and rise of global corporations: Nike, Shell, MacDonald's and Nestlé. Each of them has been accused of exploiting the silent thousands in the developing world to make better profits for the people at the top. We cannot trust the media as virtually all publications in the world are owned by one of five multi-national corporations. The media lied to us about the Gulf War, but are we much better: if we hadn't been in the habit of buying the papers to read about her life, would the Princess have been chased by the photographers in Paris?

Whom can you trust? The Church? Many of us see its vast wealth and its reluctance to be anything other than rooted in the past. It's probably the most conservative and cautious institution in the world, the last place where you could expect to find change and progress.

God is not an institution. He's not a liar, cheat or self-centred power fiend. He is personal. It has taken hundreds of years for the Church to grow up, during which time it has managed to do more to hide God's personality than it has to reveal it. The old traditions and political strategies have taken it far away from the original plan.

Look at the Bible and you will see something different. You will see a man, one who came to be vulnerable. One who came to suffer and to serve, to love and have friends as well as to change our lives forever. He was not afraid to stand up to the institutions, and he didn't hold back on telling the people who had turned knowing God into a power struggle that they were wrong and sinful. Jesus was not afraid to deliver one of the most radical political messages of all time in the Sermon on the Mount, and he came as a human being who eventually was killed by other human beings in the most cruel way imaginable.

Looking at the Bible we see a personal God who came to earth and was weak and vulnerable, yet who also triumphed over the institutions. He reached out to people, healing them and giving them hope. Later the Bible shows us the way the early Church did things; they didn't form a clique and decide to function as an institution, instead they were a living organism, a group who were beaten and even killed but who loved each other, who loved the world and who served the people. Before they were called Christians they were called the 'people of the way' because of their lifestyle and commitment to expressing what they understood of our 'personal' God.

Some would say that the worst thing that ever happened to the Christian faith was the conversion of Emperor Constantine. He declared Christianity the official religion of the Roman world and almost overnight it stopped being a subversive society and became a tool for selfish personal advancement – Christianity became a badge to wear that got you into the right clubs. The trouble was that God never went for the right clubs, he always went for the wrong ones that were full of the poor, lost and sick. That's the kind of person he is – the kind who would come as a humble carpenter from Nazareth instead of an influential religious fat cat from Jerusalem.

I'm not inviting you to join a political institution, but a group of people who are trying to follow a man. Although Jesus was rich in the sense that he owned the universe, he became poor. That's who we're looking to for guidance and instructions, to change the world by finishing what he started.

BOB'S STORY

I was born in Wimbledon and brought up in and around South-west London. I came from a dysfunctional family and as a result of problems at home I became behaviourally disturbed as a child. I got kicked out of various schools, and at the age of fifteen left school altogether with no qualifications. I couldn't even read or write properly.

When I was sixteen I joined the British Army and became 24589133 Gunner Byrne, Royal Artillery. I was based in the Midlands and visited Gibraltar. The only active service I saw was in bar room brawls with other squaddies and local civvies. I ended up in army prison, serving four short army prison sentences before getting dishonourable discharge because of my violent behaviour.

I had liked the army; it gave vent to my aggression. I thought you were meant to fight, but they were too fussy about who you did it with. I felt hurt and rejected because of my childhood and I felt hurt and rejected by the army. I joined a gang of skinheads, drank too much, got involved with drugs, slept around, lived in squats, and became a thief and drug dealer to pay for my habit, leading me on to frequent trouble with the police.

For several years I lived in a drink and drugs haze. Life was violent and confused. Because I was hurting inside, I tried to be hard on the outside. I've been stabbed in the stomach with a screwdriver. I have ten stitches in my head and five in my mouth from when I got done with an iron bar. I've been stabbed in the wrist with a broken bottle. I've been thrown through two pub windows and been in a coma on two occasions. I have also done these sorts of things to others. I was filled with hate and anger. What I really wanted, but didn't know it, was love.

At the age of twenty-one, I found myself on the run from the police and selling drugs to students in Oxford. I overdosed myself and made myself very ill. A Christian woman got me to the hospital and a Christian doctor pumped my stomach. They didn't know anything about each other, but they both said to me, 'Jesus loves you!' As I was having my stomach pumped out, I had this strange experience that God was real and that he was there with me. I can't make it sound rational because it wasn't – I just knew God was there.

They pump your stomach out, but they can't

pump your head. All night long I sat up in bed, stoned out of my brains and all I could hear over and over again was 'Jesus loves you, Jesus loves you'. I wanted to know that love in my life.

The next day when the doctors came on their round, my doctor gave me a little card with a poem printed on it. She said: 'I was praying for you last night and God said to give you this.' Then she left. The poem was 'Footprints in the Sand'. The poem speaks of how when we feel most alone, that's often when God is carrying us.

I read the poem and began to cry. I couldn't remember the last time I'd cried. I just wept and wept and wept. An hour later, the woman who had got me to the hospital came to see how I was doing. I was still crying. She asked what I was going to do and I said I was going to give myself up to the police in London. She said she would drive me there.

We stopped at a petrol station on the M40 and she got out the little book: *Journey into Life*. The book explained what it meant to become a Christian and at the end of the book there was a prayer for those who wanted to ask Jesus into their lives. I prayed the prayer and at that point I believe God forgave me all my sins and gave me a new start.

The police didn't see things quite the way God did and soon I found myself in prison. I did a sentence of two years, two months and one day. I'd been in prison before but this time it was different – God was with me. I learnt to read and write properly and took some exams. When I came out I studied Social Sciences for a couple of years and wanted to be a social worker. However, God had different plans for my life.

I got a job at a church in Battersea that had just been planted by a well-known church called Holy Trinity Brompton. I worked for St Mark's for four years. I did practical work for the church, worked with people with problems, male and female prostitutes and drug addicts. I also led services and preached. I met a girl called Debra who came from a totally different background to me, and we got married in 1991.

I felt God was calling me to ordained ministry in the Church of England, and put myself forward for the long process of selection. I eventually got through that and went on to do a degree at Oak Hill College.

I was ordained in 1995 and served a four-year curacy at St Stephen's Church, Tonbridge, Kent. Recently I have taken up a new post running one church in Coxheath, near Maidstone, and planting another church in a new residential and industrial area called Kings Hill.

We have two children, Ruth aged five and Lily who is nearly three. My life is so very different now. I love working with young people and find great joy in helping them to avoid the mistakes I made. In the years that have passed, God has been faithful to the promise he first made to me that first day: 'Jesus loves you.' He has proved his love to me in so many different ways and his love has set me free from the past.

Rev. Bob Byrne

3

God is Father

For many of us today the word 'father' isn't a very good word. Our experience may have been of a violent or abusive father, or perhaps one that simply wasn't there emotionally – too preoccupied with work or the TV to take any real interest in us. The trouble is that 'father' is a word that is used to describe God. A lot. Throughout the Book, and especially in the New Testament, we read about the Creator of heaven and earth, the most powerful force in the universe, and we're told to call him 'Dad'.

But Jesus made a point of giving us some clues to help us work out what our Father in heaven is like.

Jesus continued: 'There was a man who had two sons. The younger one said to his father, "Father, give me my share of the estate." So he divided his property between them.'

Jesus was dead keen on using stories to get his point across. Some of them were sad, some happy, but all were about everyday situations that the people he was telling them to would have understood. Kicking off this story with the sentences we've just read was one of the most shocking openings he could have chosen. It was the custom for a father's wealth to be shared out among his sons when he was dead. In asking for his slice of the pie there and then, while the old man was very much still alive and kicking, the subject of the story was delivering a shocker along the lines of 'Oi Pops. I can't wait for you to snuff it . . .' The reaction from the crowd would have been one of utter shock and disgust. But they would have gone even more mental when they heard the next line about the dad dividing things equally between the two boys. Not only did the cheeky son not get what he deserved – which was a quick slap and a kick up the butt – but he got more: he was given something he did not earn.

'Not long after that, the younger son got together all he had, set off for a distant country and there squandered his wealth in wild living. After he had spent everything, there was a severe famine in that whole country, and he began to be in need. So he went and hired himself out to a citizen of that country, who sent him to his fields to feed pigs. He longed to fill his stomach with the pods that the pigs were eating, but no one gave him anything.'

So after he got his share he went on a little wander and ended up miles away in a distant country. Perhaps he had only planned on going somewhere close to home, but eventually he found himself far away from anything familiar. Jesus made it clear that the consequences of his decision to live for himself soon caught up with him. The Bible has a word for this: it's sin – living away from our heavenly Father, choosing to go along with our own plans instead of his. Some people think that they only mean to go a little way with sin, but the nature of it means that it doesn't take long for us to end up, like the cheeky son, far away in a distant land.

But it wasn't all bad – he had a laugh. At the start it must have been a bit of a ball, perhaps he was one of the big men in town with a big wad to spend and a desire to have as much fun as possible. Sadly it didn't just end there – his fast living had a payback. It's just the same with sin: of course it's fun (if it wasn't then why would we do it in the first place?), but the fun is always followed by a set of consequences.

If the crowd had been into the story until this point, they would have gone ballistic when they heard what happened next. For a good Jewish lad to end up looking after pigs – an animal so low and unclean that they would not even want to touch, let alone eat it – would have been the ultimate disgrace. As he scrabbled round in the pen, desperate to have whatever leftovers there were after the pigs' dinner, he simply could not have got any lower.

'When he came to his senses, he said, "How many of my father's hired men have food to spare, and here I am starving to death! I will set out and go back to my father and say to him: Father, I have sinned against heaven and against you. I am no longer worthy to be called your son; make me like one of your hired men." So he got up and went to his father.'

When he got to the place of realising that he had nothing, then even the option of living like a servant in his father's house was preferable to the reality of his present situation. As he makes his way back he works on his speech. Like any child he knew how to get round his parents, and his heart-rending words were designed to get the best result – to be allowed back as a servant. You can almost hear him rehearsing his emotional speech: 'Father, I have sinned against heaven and against you [fall to knees]. I am no longer worthy to be called your son [sob heartily], make me like one of your hired men [fling self to dad's feet and kiss them].' He certainly didn't deserve such generosity: after all, in taking his father's inheritance

GOD IS FATHER

early he had backed out of the family and effectively
wished him dead.

> 'But while he was still a long way off, his father
> saw him and was filled with compassion for him;
> he ran to his son, threw his arms around him and
> kissed him.'

How did his dad see him when he was so far off? I
think that the text implies that the father was looking
out for him, that he somehow hoped his son would
return. Again Jesus followed on by chucking in some
social dynamite; no respectable Jewish farmer would
have run anywhere, let alone to reach a wayward ex-
son. If ever he had needed to have run somewhere he
would have had servants to do it for him, but instead
he hitched up his long flowing robes and legged it
towards his boy. In suggesting that God was capable
of forgetting his dignity in favour of getting closer to
one of his children Jesus was turning all the tradition-
ally held views of God upside down. He challenged
the established order of things and forced people to
think again about the boxes into which they had
placed God.

Jesus described the dad as being full of compassion.
In the original Greek version that reads more like his
guts were being ripped out, so intense was the passion
he felt for his child. He demonstrated his love through
hugs and kisses in a way that no one listening would

have expected. Still, the son seems kind of oblivious to this as he starts his speech:

> 'The son said to him, "Father, I have sinned against heaven and against you. I am no longer worthy to be called your son."
>
> 'But the father said to his servants, "Quick! Bring the best robe and put it on him. Put a ring on his finger and sandals on his feet. Bring the fattened calf and kill it. Let's have a feast and celebrate. For this son of mine was dead and is alive again; he was lost and is found." So they began to celebrate.'

I know that I handle things a bit like the son; if I've fallen out with someone and I've got it in mind to try and make it up, then I'll put some work into preparing exactly what I'm going to say. I'll often be so keen to get my words out that I'll forget to pay any attention to what they're doing or saying. In fact, when I was younger and I'd done something wrong I'd often make up two speeches: one for my mum and one for my dad. The one for my mum would involve giving her a hug and telling her how scared I was that Dad would be angry. I'd then go next door and chat with Dad about Mum being on the warpath and suggest we wash the car together. It worked every time.

That's what the son was trying to do – to persuade

his dad to take him back. He thought he'd have to work hard to get back in with his father, but he wasn't even allowed to finish his speech. The most surprising thing about the whole story is that the father immediately demands that the son have a robe, ring and sandals. This wasn't because he was looking a little shoddy, but because they were symbols of sonship – the tokens that told everyone you were a valued and much loved son.

And so the celebrations begin, just like they do whenever any of us turn back to God. How do we know this? Again, Jesus told us; he said that there is more rejoicing in heaven over one sinner who repents than over ninety-nine righteous people who don't need to repent. So this is the deal – the son coming back to the loving father is the way it can be for each of us.

'Meanwhile, the older son was in the field. When he came near the house, he heard music and dancing. So he called one of the servants and asked him what was going on. "Your brother has come," he replied, "and your father has killed the fattened calf because he has him back safe and sound."

'The older brother became angry and refused to go in. So his father went out and pleaded with him. But he answered his father, "Look! All these years I've been slaving for you and never disobeyed your orders. Yet you never gave me even a young goat so I could celebrate with my friends. But when this son of yours who has squandered your property with prostitutes comes home, you kill the fattened calf for him!" '

It's easy to see that where the younger son didn't understand just how strong and forgiving the father's love was, the elder son was just as confused but in a different way. In his mind he'd earned the right to have a big fuss made of him; he had been working hard for all that time and had never broken the rules in the way his younger brother had. The father soon puts him straight:

' "My son," the father said, "you are always with me, and everything I have is yours. But we had to celebrate and be glad, because this brother of yours was dead and is alive again; he was lost and is found." '

(Luke 15:11–32)

This is a tragedy – the elder son never needed to slave away to earn the good stuff, for as Dad tells him, everything was his already. This is not unusual for us human beings; there are plenty of people who go along thinking that by keeping up a good record of attendance they are earning themselves a decent position in heaven. Jesus's story makes it clear that it's not like this. Just like the father in the story, God loves us even before we start to do good things for him. He loves us when we're bad as well as when we're good. He loves us when we break the rules and when we keep them, but he doesn't love us because of this; God loves us because it's his nature and he cannot help himself.

I'm not saying that we should not put in the hours working for God's purpose – far from it. But all our efforts are meaningless if they're done just to earn his favour. Our obedience to the Father is an act of love, returning the unconditional love he has for us.

There are three sons in this story: the younger one who went away and came back, the elder one who was always there but was away in his heart, and the son who tells the story – Jesus. He knew what it meant to be loved by his Father and he knew what it meant to be accepted and cared for. He wants us to follow his lead and sign up for the same kind of relationship with the Father that he has.

We know more about prodigal fathers in this age than about prodigal sons, and this story makes a huge impact on us, showing exactly what God is like: passionate, forgiving, generous and strong. He doesn't care that he breaks the rules of what we may think a father is like. God doesn't swear at us or cut us down in public. He doesn't drink too much and come home violent. He doesn't get annoyed when we ask him for some time and he doesn't go quiet when we ask him how he's feeling. He doesn't leave, let down or abuse. He won't shy away when you go to hug him and he doesn't have favourites. He doesn't wish we were someone else and he doesn't want out. He's not a cheat, a liar or a slob and he won't push us away.

CHRIS'S STORY

There are two types of vicars' kids: those who
are hung up about it and those who aren't.
Which one you are depends a lot on the attitude
of the old parentals. Fortunately, I was brought
up in a family where being part of a church
leader's family was no big deal, especially as I
was the balanced middle kid with an older sister
and younger brother. We were all very different
and my parents encouraged us to be ourselves.
So when I'd get picked up from parties at the
age of six and my mum would be told, 'I thought
he would behave better being a vicar's son',
she'd usually side with me rather than with
them, knowing that just 'cos Dad was a vicar it
didn't mean that I was going to be better
behaved (it usually means the opposite).

I grew up saying grace at meals, learning how
to colour in the disciples and having weird
missionaries staying the night. Something about
being a missionary meant that they never
bothered to lock the bathroom door, so you'd
always walk in on them getting ready for bed,
and then not be able to look them in the eye at
breakfast the next morning.

God was always around. We were taught to

call him Father, ask him for help and cry to him when we were scared. We expected that he'd be exactly like Jesus had told us and showed us through the Bible.

I think most people who have parents who lead churches get viewed quite strangely by the rest of the people in the congregation – always being compared to their mum or dad. Many of the people in the church I grew up in thought I would believe the same, act the same and have the same opinions as my dad. But my parents had encouraged us to think, do and believe things for ourselves. I knew that everyone thought I was just doing the church thing because of my dad – but I knew it was all real to me. Anyway, when I was fourteen I went along to a big rally and heard someone explain about Jesus dying for me. I knew about giving your life to God already, but I wanted him to know that I meant it, so I did one of those public up-to-the-front-at-the-end-of-the-meeting-here's-my-life-Jesus things. I went home and told my parents and we were all happy.

As I was going through my teenage years I didn't seriously think about rebelling against God. It never seemed worth it – what was the point when God was so good and wanted the best life for me? But I did rebel against being a vicar's son – I've tried to purge the planet of all photos of me at that time (unfortunately there are a few still out there) – but take it from me, I looked a real sight most of the time. I'd have to sneak out the back door to go to parties because of what my mum would say about how I was dressed. It was always a shock to people I was a vicar's son – but my parents never stopped me or told me dressing like this was wrong. That was a vital lesson – not to get confused between rebelling against the expectations people had of me and sticking two fingers up at God. I rebelled against one and adored the other, and I think the ability to make that distinction helped me thrive.

There was a group of us who were all Christians. We'd go to parties together and try and keep each other in line. They were good, life-wise Christians too and we shared a lot, so much that I don't think I'd have survived on my own.

Worship was an important thing for me. It's not that the church was cool or full of trendies, in fact we often had that service written in 1662 and murdered psalms every week. I can't remember any talks (sorry, Dad), but when I was about fifteen I had heard someone speaking in tongues. I remember being both freaked out and completely intrigued. I knew I wanted it and started praying for it in my room at night. I began to really enjoy being with God – feeling him within touchable distance – and just kept getting overwhelmed. Being loved this much by Jesus did good things to my heart, and I would spend ages praying, reading my Bible and singing (quietly in case anyone should hear) in tongues. This would all happen in my room, and his Spirit would pick me up and take a hold.

At the same time I was doing my A Levels and loving RE. I was a bit worried about this, especially as I thought everyone would tell me that I was going to be a vicar, which was the last thing in the world I wanted to do. Being a vicar's kid means that you've got to be your own person. Still I loved having the opportunity to look into God's stuff, who he was, how we might really know him and what difference it could make. I was also mouthy and loved spouting my opinions, which made RE even more fun. As this was the subject I really enjoyed I applied to study theology – talking about God – at university. Some people started trying to dissuade me, saying how everyone who studies theology loses their faith, but this made me even more determined. I mean, how stupid is it to assume that the Christian faith can't stand up to a detailed look? If it couldn't, I thought, well who wants to believe in something that weak? I knew Jesus was true, but wanted to know more and to be able to tell people more about him.

My faith did stand up, and I even went back for more, completing a second theology degree. I worked at the House of Commons for a while, and then did something that I really wanted to do – trained to become a vicar. Somewhere in the middle of it all I met my most wonderful wife, and have got more and more excited, more and more overwhelmed by how and why this God loves us. I've been more and more inspired to get the news of this God and his Kingdom out there. There's not anything or anyone who is and does as God is and does.

Chris Russell

4

God is Creator

Now I've never had any myself so maybe I'm not one to talk, but it seems clear to me that people have children for all sorts of reasons. Some do it because they're bored, some because they're drunk, some because they want something to play with. But as well as knowing that a child is for life and not just for Christmas, most of the rest of us also know, however deep down, that the best reason behind the urge to create a wee baby is a love between two people which makes them want to create someone whom they can share their love with. Most people see children as an investment – perhaps not financially, but certainly emotionally. Parents tend to be into the idea of lavishing their love on the nippers and seeing them grow over the years, becoming people who in their own right can pass on love and carry on the tradition. Something inside us draws us to this; the need to know love and create is as basic as our need for warmth and shelter.

It's a simple step to take here from talking about children to talking about God. You see, some people believe we are here by chance, the result of a random series of bangs, collisions and slugs crawling out of the sea. But our need to recreate, and the longing for a sense of purpose, are hints that we too were originally created by something or someone else. It was either an accident or part of a plan – and even when I was a fuming atheist I just couldn't get my head around the idea that we existed only by chance. The thought that I might not be anything more than just a simple blip in history – now you see me now you don't – the idea that my life was just another grain of sand in a desert of emptiness was not something that made me happy. There had to be more, I thought; there had to be a reason why.

It was only when I started talking to Christians and reading the Bible that I discovered that we were made for a purpose, that there was a point to it all. I found out that we were made by a Creator who did it not because he was forced to, but because he wanted to have a relationship with us. Just as parents have children so that they can give them love, so God created us so that we could receive and enjoy his love.

The big book for us Christians kicks off with a clear message explaining why we were created in the first place. It says that God made us 'in his image', in other words that we have inherited bits of his character. The whole of the Bible screams out the same story: God is personal. He is interested in us, he loves us and wants us to get closer to him. The Creator cannot therefore be an impersonal force; God cannot be an 'it' that doesn't care for us or a mysterious collection of gases that we can never understand or communicate with. He has got personality and character and we can get to know him. Sure the Bible is full of weird and wonderful stories, of characters and people so varied and unique that one of them even took to burying his underpants in a wall (believe me, it's true), but throughout it all we see God, the star of the show – constant throughout.

In his first letter John describes God perfectly: 'God is love'. The rest of the Bible backs that up, giving us a clear picture of a God who didn't create us as a bizarre experiment only to place us back onto the shelf once he had played with us for a while. As we were made for his pleasure, we were made to have relationship with him. Because of that our hearts will always long to be brought back home to him.

The name of the book of Genesis also means 'beginnings', which seems fairly appropriate seeing as how it starts the whole Bible thing off. This book of beginnings starts out with a chapter titled 'The

Beginning', and with the words 'In the beginning God created . . .' The clever ones amongst you will have noticed a common theme there, and we can all be fairly sure that the story of the world – our story – begins with God. But even before we all began God was around. We later find out that he's the kind of guy who's bigger than that whole beginning and ending thing, that he always has been around and always will be around. For us bods who have a very real sense of when we start and when we finish this can be quite confusing, but it is also the solution to an awful lot of head scratching. We've spent centuries wondering how the world started, how the galaxy was formed and how the universe came into existence. Like that game when every answer is met by the question 'why?' we can keep on trying to trace back our beginnings to the nth degree. But with God it's different. Believing that he was there first and that he created it all in the first place gives us the chance to make sense of it all.

In the Bible's telling of the story of how it all began we see that God works through things steadily; first he creates light, then sky and water, land and seas, sun, moon and stars. Then come fish to fill the seas and birds to fill the air, after which come the animals. On the final day of his creative burst he decided to make human beings 'in our image, in our likeness'. Only by creating man and woman can he express the full extent of his beauty, and only when he has shown us just how creative he is can we begin to understand what it means for us to have been created in his image.

After this, so the story goes, God was pleased with what he saw and he rested. I think it's interesting that according to this, our first full day on the planet was a day of rest. This seems odd for us busy people, but perhaps it's another subtle hint about the reason why we're here in the first place; could it be that, instead of our main aim being to earn as much cash as possible or to leave as big an empire as we can, the reason why we are here is to spend time with God, to discover and develop our relationship with him and others?

You might be getting a bit excited by all this talk of God creating everything in six days flat. Surely we grew out of all that stuff years ago? Well, some people believe that it all happened from Monday to Saturday, but many Christians believe that while the proportions are right, it is more likely that this Scripture is talking symbolically of six chunks of time, rather than six blocks of twenty-four hours. I think that science tells us more about creation than the Bible does, and that it can give us a much more detailed picture of how we got here than we can find in Scripture. But, what science cannot answer is the question that could easily be a subtitle of the Bible, *Why Did We Get Here?* Science attempts to tell us how, only the Bible can tell us why. The answer to this is the truth that we all yearn for. It's what gives our lives meaning and purpose, and a life without knowing means missing out.

To see that we were made in the image of a creator God helps us to explain all the creativity that can be found within us. When Michelangelo painted the Sistine Chapel or sculpted the boy David, when Mozart wrote his symphonies or when chart legend Meatloaf penned his 1975 classic 'I Would Do Anything For Love' (yes, I am a fan), each of them was expressing something of the nature of God. The fact that our creativity is inherited from the ultimate Creator goes some way to explaining why we place so much importance and give so much respect to those who can create.

I was fifteen when I became a Christian. I can remember that one of the things that made me so happy was the fact that at last I knew I wasn't alone and adrift in the universe. I wasn't just the product of some hanky-panky late one night in my parents' bed, nor was I Mike Pilavachi just because the right sperm had reached the egg at the right time, beating all the other sperm to it. It wasn't by chance that I was here and I wasn't going to disappear as soon as I was dead. Finally I knew that my life had purpose and I felt great. I knew that while I was in my mother's womb God knit me together, and that even before then, even before Mum and Dad played their part in the whole Mike P story, God had me on his mind.

These are strange days; fear and confusion are top of the bill as we try to make sense of the world around us. One of the biggest reasons that our society today is full of people living with the horror of anorexia, bulimia, alcoholism and drug abuse, as well as those who self-harm and are suicidal, is because, although we're stuffed up to the eyeballs with material wealth and possessions, we're running critically low on a sense of purpose. Are we just here for seventy years and that's it? Is there nothing more to life than the here and now? If this is all we have to live for, then there's no wonder that the strain begins to show.

The thing that certainly puts a smile on my face is the knowledge that we are here for a reason and that we find a reason for living as opposed to a reason for existing when we discover a life with God.

Some old chap named Rousseau said that 'most men live lives of quiet desperation'. I think he had a point; for many of us the weeks drift by, separated only by the snippets of time we get for ourselves at the weekends, and it all blurs together into a mishmash of months, of two-week holidays that are longed for from one end of the year to the next. The decades slip by, grey with memory and low on meaning. We look for things to brighten it up for us, but it is only through getting to know the God who made us for a purpose as a personal friend that we can find freedom.

CRAIG'S STORY

I used to dream of receiving a knighthood. Sir Craig Borlase had a lovely ring to it. I wasn't kidding myself; I didn't think I'd get it for great works of charity, just for being really, really rich. I'm glad to say things have changed.

My father was unreliable. His relationship with my mum ended when I was in nappies and throughout my first decade any contact we had came when I visited him during school holidays. He married, had a son, and by the time I was eleven our relationship had become so 'non' that it was easier to forget about him than suffer the pain of being continually let down. After one particularly bad visit I said that I didn't want to talk to him. 'He knows where to find me if he wants me' was what he told my mum on the phone when she gave him the news. That was the last I heard from him.

My mum found healing in the church, and I grew up knowing God. Having always loved attention I did a bit of drama at church. People began opening up to the Holy Spirit, and so did I. I began to believe my own hype and to think that my praying, prophesying and shaking made me special. Still, church was good: I felt accepted there, although I hated spending the week at school where no one really understood what I was about. To my mind they were sinners and were to be avoided at all costs.

At the age of nine I had gained a step-dad and a couple of step-brothers. One lived with us and was going through his own troubles which didn't make for a very cosy home-life. Despite that, as I forgot about my dad and concentrated on the good things around me, I was pretty happy with things.

It didn't last. Things seemed to go a bit wrong when I was fifteen. Home was hosting arguments you could set your watch by; I seemed to be losing my status at church (those offers to get on stage were disappearing); I started thinking about my father (whom I hadn't thought about for three years); the buzz of receiving from the Holy Spirit didn't seem to be having any impact on my life.

Actually, not everything was going wrong, for I started to hang around with people from school, getting into the good times and trying to be a little bit naughty. I struggled like this for a few months, trying to get back into church, but eventually it became clear that the world was spoiling my enjoyment of God, and God was spoiling my enjoyment of the world. 'Go,' said my youth leader. 'We'll be here when you want to come back.'

I quit church and found friends, drugs, literature and girls. This carried on when I got to college, but there I was faced with harder drugs, less study and a singled-minded intention to enjoy myself. After a year I felt ill and through a couple of great mates I started being friends with Jesus again.

Strangely enough, it feels as though this was when all the work began – this was when things stopped making sense and I began searching. I felt like this was the wrong way round – aren't you supposed to get low, start searching and then find God? Once I was back at church I realised that I loved the friends I had made in the previous three years and I loved bits of the culture that I had thrown myself into, but my old version of Christianity was telling me that these things were wrong.

The thought of selling up and returning to the Christian Ghetto made me sad: I felt like I had tasted life, I didn't want it to go stale. Thankfully I found a group of friends who hung out on the fringes of church culture who were supportive and loving. They loved to be creative and they valued friendship. It was just what I needed: the chance to be Christian Craig Mk II, a very different model from the teenage prototype. Leaving church brought me closer to God. I lost the interest in hype and being a Holy Spirit junky. Instead of begging God to come down and give me a supernatural fireworks display, or ignoring my hell-bound friends, I found that what I valued most was genuine friendship – with God and others.

The stuff with my father is still the same – perhaps it's the thorn in my flesh – but I've learnt not to try and compensate for the feelings by trying to get people to notice me. Although I was a bit of a fool for a time, hurting myself and others in ways I would never want to repeat, I believe that God, in his mysterious ways, helped me lose my religion. It did me the world of good.

Craig Borlase

5

The Scandal of God

Think of Christianity and I'll bet most people will think about Christmas. In will come mental pictures of gold-embossed cards, carols that make you yawn and some weird story about a bloke on a donkey with stabilisers. Of course, if you've done your homework you will be thinking about Jesus being born in a stable with old and dignified wise men standing next to young and enthusiastic shepherds. You might like to chuck in a few animals, maybe a big-eyed cow and a couple of soft sheep (all odour free, of course). Jesus in his little white nightie would be sleeping soundly, or perhaps staring knowingly about him. There may be a scattering of snow outside, but inside the people, animals and presents are all surrounded by a warming glow that suggests a beautiful family on their way to a beautiful life.

It's true: Jesus was born in a stable, but it wasn't quite like this. The circumstances were kind of different. A few years ago, when I was a youth leader I tried to rediscover the truth about the birth of Jesus. The church was at one end of a reasonably sized village, and each year at Christmas the local shopkeepers helped put on a Christmas night in the high street. Basically this involved them feeding customers with mince pies, burgers and a lethal brew of mulled wine. Feeling full and a bit woozy the happy shoppers would then stroll from shop to shop, merrily purchasing whatever useless tat they didn't need and wouldn't buy when they were sober. It was a stroke of genius on the part of the shopkeepers and was something of a tradition in the village.

On this particular year our church had been asked to do what we could to put on some kind of carol singing and nativity play to entertain the village. It seemed like a great idea, and because I had run out of things to do my vicar gave me the job. Now I'd always fancied myself as a bit of a director, and ever since I had seen Sooty play Prince Charming at the Basildon Palace in *Cinderella* I knew that I wanted to go into the theatre. Working with the likes of Sooty was a long way off, but as I accepted the challenge of putting on the village play. I knew that it was the start of something big.

As the weeks of rehearsal rolled by my plans for the production grew more and more ambitious. I had started with the idea of putting it on as a mime, but when I realised that no one knew how to mime anything other than feeling their way around a glass wall, I binned the idea. Later I thought that it might be nice if we did it in the original Aramaic – the language spoken by Jesus. Again, we hit a bit of a dead end when I found out that the only languages known among the congregation were French, Spanish and enough German to order two Schnitzels and a taxi to the airport. Not one to be deterred, I decided to aim even higher. In a flash of inspiration I remembered the joy of sitting in that theatre in Basildon watching Sooty sweep the beautiful Cinderella off her feet. I decided to do what I knew would be best and went with the 'natural' idea, calling up anyone I knew who had an animal that we could borrow.

On the night of the performance we gathered in the car park of the church and went through our final checks. Instead of a donkey we had only been able to get a horse named Viper for Mary and Joseph to ride, but I was convinced that no one would notice. There had been a bit of trouble trying to track down a flock of sheep, so the three shepherds had to make do with a flock of sheep that consisted of only one goat. Still, I was sure people would get the idea.

The best thing though was the costumes. Someone in the church had made them for all the characters: Mary and Joseph, the three kings, the three shepherds and the angel Gabriel. They all looked excellent, although if you looked hard it wasn't difficult to see what order she had made them in. The three kings were immaculately fitted out in robes that could have come straight from a movie set, while the shepherds were a bit shabbier. This kind of made sense though, apart from the fact that one of them looked as though he was wearing clothes borrowed from a child half his age. What I did notice, however, was the angel Gabriel. All the white muslin had been used up on the kings, so Gabe's outfit had to be made from old material that was going spare. Unfortunately, the only old material that was going spare was an old duvet cover paying homage to Darth Vader. It was a bit of a shame, but as the angel (played by a lovely man named George) walked about the car park with his cape flowing behind him, all I could think of was that I was glad the *Star War's* villain hadn't worn sandals as well.

It went wrong when I noticed that Mary, Joseph and Gabriel all wore glasses. While I could forgive the odd sandal here and there, glasses were a different thing altogether. It just didn't look right, and despite the fact that Mary told me she was blind without them, I managed to persuade them to do it for the sake of the play.

Being without her glasses made Mary nervous, but not nearly as nervous as being on a horse. As she climbed on the back of Viper, she remembered why it had been years since she had ridden a horse. She shook as though they were galloping even though the horse had not moved an inch.

Still, confidence was high enough and we walked down the hill towards the high street. I marched on ahead next to the carol singers who were warming up with a bit of 'Good King Wenceslas'. As we prepared to turn left into the high street I looked back to check how things were going. Badly. There were only two shepherds and no flock.

'Stop,' I shouted. 'Where is Shepherd number three?'

Silence. Everyone turned and looked. Eventually, to my horror I saw Shepherd number three at the end of the road pulling the goat's lead as if he were on the losing side in a tug of war. What was worse was that the goat was chewing its way rapidly through a selection of some villager's prized winter pansies. The two other shepherds ran to help and they all pushed the goat as hard as they could towards us at the front. The goat didn't like this too much and trotted ahead making it clear how much he didn't want to be a sheep. Shepherd number three felt likewise and the two were in a strop with each other all night.

Turning the corner into the high street we came to our first stop at the Post Office. Here was a decent crowd of people already enjoying the tray of mince pies and mulled wine that was on offer on the table outside the shop. Our carol singers sang, people looked happy and the horse decided to relieve himself not only up the side of the shop doorway but onto the tray of pies itself. I was embarrassed and the postmaster was angry.

We carried on singing 'Silent Night' as we legged it up the road. Arriving at the butcher's I turned around and noticed that this time it was Shepherd number two who was missing with the goat. I looked across and they were having another argument. Just when things started to get heated Shepherd number two picked up the goat by its legs and slung it around his neck. The goat was not happy. It was not the kind of effect I was after.

At that point I looked around and saw that we were minus two kings.

'Where are Kings two and three?' I asked King number one.

He looked embarrassed and pointed to the butcher's. Standing in a queue for burgers were Kings one and two. Calmly I walked up to them and enquired as to why they felt it was appropriate for two kings to be queuing for junk food.

'You don't understand, Mike,' said King number one. 'I'm the burger King.'

I didn't laugh.

By this stage I was upset. Everything had gone wrong; Shepherd number three was in a huff at the back of the carol singers, Shepherd number two was wrestling the goat to the ground, Kings number two and three were trying to wipe the ketchup off their robes, Joseph was trying to calm Mary down after the horse had started to walk back towards the mince pies and small children were crying at the sight of the angel Gabriel. I sat down on the bench at the crossroads and turned to the angel.

'George,' I told him. 'This is not how it was supposed to be.' The angel Gabriel looked at me and said, 'Mike, isn't this more like the first Christmas than what you intended it to be?'

I stopped and thought. He was right; what I had planned was a sanitised version of the birth of Jesus, one without the muck and reality that would have been there. According to the Bible the very first Christmas was very different to the one that I had wanted to stage. It happened when a virgin who was engaged to be married was visited by an angel and told that she was pregnant. Joseph was still up for marrying her when he found out, but planned to divorce her quietly after a while as he wasn't really sure that she was telling the truth. Then the angel appeared to him as well and confirmed that it was a miraculous conception. Despite the fact that both believed that she was still a virgin, people not surprisingly would still have questioned Mary's story, and as a result Jesus was born with one of the greatest social handicaps of the day: rumours of illegitimacy.

In the final weeks of her pregnancy Mary had to go with Joseph away from their home town and back to the place of his birth. Bethlehem was over one hundred miles away from Nazareth; no trains, no planes, no automobiles; just lots of walking and a donkey. They were homeless as all the hotels had been comprehensively pre-booked, only able to find a stable for the birth. Perhaps you might think that a palace would have been too obvious a place for a saviour to be born, but surely God could have come up with something better than a stable. Wouldn't a nice semi-detached have been more appropriate?

The only people there to celebrate his birth were the kings (or wise men as they are sometimes known) and the shepherds. At first you could be forgiven for thinking that the wise men might sound like decent sorts, but at that time they would have earned no respect at all for the simple fact that they were foreigners. What's more, in Israel the kind of people who were shepherds were the kind who couldn't do anything else. They were the dregs, but even within their profession there was another hierarchy. Guess who was at the bottom? The night shift. That's what these shepherds were: so inept that they couldn't even get a decent job in the lowest sector of employment. They were muppets of the highest order. The most shocking, amazing and wonderful thing about Christmas is this, however: that in baby Jesus God became a human being.

The story of the first Christmas is that God became like one of us so that we could be rescued from our failure and our sin. God became like those he created, like the most vulnerable ones in his creation. Can you imagine what it must have been like for the Creator and Ruler of the universe to become a baby? Can you imagine the indignity of being dependent on people for everything in your life? Feeding, changing, soiling and vomiting are hardly the sort of things you would expect the Almighty to want to be doing. What's more, can you imagine why God should so value you and me that he would choose to do this?

This is the message of Christianity; it is a mad scandal, one that can only be considered rubbish or truth. It is so extreme that it is impossible to be neutral about it. One of the words we use at Christmas is 'Emmanuel'. This word crops up in the Old Testament book of Isaiah when the writer predicts that one of the names of this miraculous baby would be Emmanuel, meaning 'God with us'. And so we come to the heart of the Christmas story: God with us. When the human race turned away from God, when we made a mess of the whole thing and hurt each other, when our selfishness had become extreme, God didn't stand back and let us suffocate and pay for our own punishment. The message of the stable is that God stepped in, that he made himself accessible to us. God made the first move.

JEANNIE'S STORY

Although my parents were not churchgoers they sent me to Sunday school for a couple of years when I was eight. The only thing I remember was being taught that if I told lies then I would get black spots on my heart, and if I crossed myself before going over a road, I was less likely to get run over. With this helpful spiritual knowledge under my belt, I approached puberty.

When I was a teenager I used to spend hours wondering what was the point of life. I wanted to know what it was all about and why I existed. I used to write morbid poetry to make sense of it all. I remember asking my mum when I was fourteen why hot cross buns had crosses on them and what they had to do with Easter. My mum came from a non-practising Catholic family and my dad came from a Spiritualist background. Neither of them had any answers for me.

I married Ken when I was nineteen and all these questions faded away. I was happy, and even happier when I found out at twenty-two that I was pregnant. It wasn't until I was thirty-six weeks into the pregnancy that, after poor antenatal care, I had an X-ray which showed that the baby was not going to live after it had been born. Our baby was anencephalic, which means that the skull had not formed to the usual size because the brain had not grown. It was impossible for the baby to live with such a tiny brain. No one told me the results of the X-ray and they lied to me about the health of the baby. Only Ken knew the truth, but they told him not to tell me. Instead he had to watch me go through two days of induced labour while student midwives practised their painful examinations of me knowing I would have no baby to hold at the end of it.

The horror of giving birth to a deformed dead baby, of still being a mother but having nothing to show for the thirty-six weeks of loving and nurturing of my unborn child threw my mind and emotions into chaos. I didn't fit in with my friends who had no children, and I certainly didn't fit in with those who did have them. I was repulsed by the pictures my imagination conjured up of what our baby must have looked like – we were not allowed to see our baby daughter so my imagination was probably far worse than the actual truth.

Although my concept of God was 'something somewhere', I clearly remember thinking and feeling that I was being punished by an unjust God. I shouted at the top of my voice in anger, 'I never *ever* want to know you.' An interesting statement as I never even realised at that time that anyone could know God.

I swallowed my grief as it was so difficult to grieve for someone I had never met and no one ever gave me permission to speak of my baby – they were too embarrassed. In desperation I quickly became pregnant again. This time around I formed no relationship with my unborn child. In fact, by the time I was thirty-six weeks pregnant again and had the routine X-ray, I reacted in a strange way. Seeing pictures of a perfectly formed head and body I started saying out loud over and over again, 'I'm pregnant – I'm pregnant.'

'Yes, Mrs Morgan,' said the doctors and nurses in calm voices, as if they were talking to someone stupid, 'we can see you're pregnant.'

During the rest of the pregnancy I allowed myself to believe that this baby might live. Although it was a difficult birth I was overjoyed to hold our daughter Alexandra in my arms. After ten days in hospital where I only got one hour of sleep each night as I was so anxious about my baby, I was allowed home.

Even though I was hyperactive and anxious, I was also quite confident in the hospital. As soon as I got home, exhausted, my new responsibility to keep this young baby alive suddenly hit me and threw me into an overanxious state of mind. I can remember trying to care for a screaming baby during our first night home, when nothing I did seemed to help. I slipped over the edge into hysteria as I rushed down the stairs completely out of control screaming, 'Help me – please help me.' I was put into bed where I reverted to the foetal position, sucking my thumb.

There followed a complete nervous breakdown lasting three months. For the first three weeks I was unable to make even the simplest decision. If I was asked whether I wanted a hot drink or a cold one my answer was, 'I don't know.' I was unable to do the simplest of tasks because I had no confidence. It was even impossible for me to change the sterilisation water for Alex's bottles; I was afraid I might do it wrong and she might die. I refused to take any of the medication that was prescribed as I was convinced that Ken and the doctor were trying to poison me. After three weeks the doctor was ready to commit me to a psychiatric hospital but the shock of returning to a hospital environment snapped me out of the manic stage and I started to accept the medication offered me. The doctor introduced me to a Christian who ran courses called 'Relaxation for Living'. I didn't know it at the time, but she belonged to a prayer group that had started to pray for me. Years later I realised that God had used these two Christians to bring me through this time of agony. After three months I gradually became well again and had a positive attitude.

A couple of years later we decided to have another child, and another girl was born – Joanna. Unlike the rest of us in the family she had blonde curly hair, and as far as births go it was great. Due to a medical problem I was sterilised a year later, and as we didn't want any more children this seemed like the best thing to do. When Joanna was two years and three months old tragedy struck. We had a swimming pool in the garden – actually it was more like a concrete hole – four foot deep, unheated and not even filtered. Joanna never went in it – she said it was cold, 'nasty cold'. The weather had been warm at the weekend and the safety net that usually covered it was pulled back. It took two people to secure it back on and we hadn't put it back. Joanna and I had been in the garden for a while and Alex was out at a friend's house. The doorbell rang and I went in from the garden to let Alex in. As Alex and I called out Joanna's name we rushed upstairs thinking she was hiding from us. Halfway up the stairs we looked out of the window to see her body floating in the pool.

When I reached the hospital and they were fighting to save Joanna's life, a big black momma of a nurse held me in her arms to comfort me.

'God is punishing me because I was sterilised,' I told her.

She pulled away from me and looked at me. 'Honey,' she said, 'our God doesn't work that way.' Those words were truth and they went inside me to the depth of my being and took away that lie. I knew she was telling the truth. As the doctors walked in to give us the prognosis I turned around to escape but there was no way out. By the look on their faces I knew it was going to be bad news. They told us that either Joanna would be a vegetable all her life or she would die within the next couple of days. For the first time since I was a little girl I said a prayer. It was simple but I knew that God heard it. 'Please, God, let her die.' If it happened to me now I would pray a different prayer, but at the time I knew what I had prayed was a good and right prayer. Bad things had happened before but nothing had ever been like this.

At that age Joanna was totally dependent on me and needed me for virtually everything throughout the day. Having her with me was like having part of my own body following me around. To be without her was like having a major part of me severed. Although I had a husband and a daughter whom I dearly loved, everything within me cried out for this child that was no longer there.

In a couple of days a vicar arrived from the local church, St Andrew's. His name was David Pytches, and as he stood in the kitchen he said the most unusual thing, 'Let's say a prayer together.' I thought you only prayed in church or at weddings or funerals, but was even more shocked by what he said next. 'Dear Jesus, please come by your presence into this kitchen.' As David reached the front door I said, 'For a vicar I think you're a very nice person, but we don't really want to be bothered with all the stuff you're saying.' He said that it was fine but that there were a lot of people praying for us because they cared about what had happened.

After that the strangest thing happened – whenever I went into the kitchen I could sense this warmth both in me and around me. I couldn't explain it, but I knew that I liked it. As the week went on we started to have some more unusual experiences. We couldn't put into words what was happening – we had no vocabulary to describe it – and all we could come up with was the idea that all these praying Christians must be emitting some kind of electricity that we were feeling. We were being comforted in our pain. I had a distinct impression of hands drawing me along to somewhere. In fact I had so many experiences of what I now know is the Holy Spirit, that if someone had told me about him then I would have immediately said that I know him.

Our closest friends were also affected by this spiritual presence. They told other friends, 'Go and see them, you will feel comforted.' This lasted up to and including Joanna's funeral day. I knew nothing about the Bible and so I didn't realise the significance of what I was saying when I told people that it was Joanna's Wedding Day. I wanted everyone to dress as if they were going to a wedding and it was the most amazing funeral I have ever been to. The crematorium chapel was full of light and lots of people from St Andrew's had come to offer us their support.

The next day I was plunged into despair. Once more I felt unable to grieve by crying. I felt guilty about what had happened and felt as if my life had no hope whatsoever. David Pytches kept on visiting us and had brought me a Bible. This really annoyed me as I had been brought up to be polite and knew that I would have to pay for it by going to church. I also desperately wanted to know where Joanna was now that she had died. We had never had her christened as we thought it would be hypocritical since we were not believers. David read me a verse from the Bible, 'Unless you change and become as a little child you can never enter the kingdom of heaven.' She was not old enough to choose – she was in the kingdom of heaven. I felt satisfied with this for a few days until I realised that I didn't know about me – was I going to heaven? Did this mean I would never see her again?

I went to church to pay for the Bible. There were so many people there that I recognised from the village but hadn't realised that they were churchgoers. Even though I had never known any, my opinion of Christians was that they were weird and out to get you. As soon as I arrived at the church I immediately felt enclosed in something that I can only describe as being like cotton wool. Later I learnt the language to describe it – it was love, love for Jesus and love from Jesus. At last I had found a place to cry and grieve. I kept coming back to the church, taking communion even though I wasn't a believer. That was where he met me in my pain; I wept and wept and no one interfered. Sometimes I felt a hand on my arm but no one stopped me crying. I felt safe to let it out there, and every Sunday I would go home red and puffy from crying. I still thought the Bible was a fairy tale and that Jesus was just a story, but I knew the Holy Spirit.

On two consecutive weeks there was a sermon about knowing Jesus. Two weeks running I asked Jesus into my life but wasn't sure if I really believed it. On the third week there was another sermon about knowing Jesus and another call to give my life to him. This time around I thought to myself either this Jesus is real or he's a lie. I knew I couldn't keep asking him into my life for the rest of time – I decided to take a risk and ask him in, believing that he would. I felt no different, just relieved that I had made a decision. The next day I woke up and felt very different, but couldn't describe how. As I went outside what I saw was incredible – it was as if all creation had a new vibrancy. It was like the first time that I wore glasses when I found out that without them I was unable to see properly. I knew what I had been missing. Everything had clarity and purpose.

The next major thing that happened in my step towards knowing Jesus was a conversation that I had with a friend of a friend. She wasn't a Christian and as we were talking one day she suggested that I have an operation to reverse my sterilisation. Almost as soon as she had said it she took it back, saying, 'I don't know why I said that; all obstetricians are butchers.' She was a nurse and the wife of an eminent surgeon, and I knew that at that time the reversal operation was only ten per cent successful.

The next day as I was walking home from school I suddenly had these two impressions in my head. One was an audible voice saying, 'Trust in me, trust in me'. The voice was big, strong, warm and kind. The other was a whining voice and I saw the serpent from the film *The Jungle Book* which was also saying, 'Trust in me'. I knew nothing of the significance of the serpent in the Bible, but it was horrible. I made a decision – I wanted to go with the warm voice and turned away from the whining voice. Immediately I was desperate to run all the way home and phone the Consultant who had carried out my operation and ask him to reverse it.

Then came my second prayer. I knelt by the sink in the bathroom and prayed, 'Please God, please give me a baby.' Later, when I talked to the Consultant, I felt hope for the first time. He explained that he had pioneered a new operation that was seventy-five per cent successful. What he didn't tell me was that he hadn't done one for a year and that he had only done four in total.

I had the operation and one year later Elizabeth (Beth) was born. When we chose her name we didn't know that it meant 'gift from God'. Whenever we went to the village shops people would come up to me and ask if this was our miracle baby. So many people had prayed for her to be conceived.

Jesus continued to heal me. At one time the healing was immediate when Alex, who was six at the time, said something that I am sure was from God. It healed all my unresolved grief about Sarah, our first baby. Over the couple of years after I had given my life to Jesus I was significantly healed of many painful memories of Joanna's death. Instead of remembering the doctors working on her, I could see how beautiful and precious she was, how much she was God's child. In time I was also healed of my massive inferiority complex, huge feelings of insecurity and a lack of self-worth and self-esteem. I became free, not bound.

I fell in love with Jesus and he became the lover of my soul. He took me from the slimy pit of hopelessness and helplessness and tenderly touched me with his love. I will never stop thanking him for all the healing he has done in my life. Through the death of Joanna seven people in our family became Christians. I believe that God used her death to bring glory to himself in a way that would have been impossible without it. I honestly believe that I would not have become a Christian had these things not happened to me. He would have come to me, but I wouldn't have received him.

I've been healed. I am being healed. I will be healed. I give glory to God through Jesus Christ – my Lord and my friend – for all that he has done. His love is the kind that will not let me go.

Jeannie Morgan

6

God and the Underdogs

So you might have got your head around the idea that Jesus's birth wasn't too great. You might even have taken on board that stuff about how God didn't just leave us to suffer the consequences of our own sin but that he made the first move. But still you might be wondering what all this Jesus fuss is about. How can a strange birth mean so much? Well, my friend, read on.

The point of Christianity is not just that God came down to earth; it's what he did and how he did it. Through not only his birth but his life, death and return to heaven Jesus completely reversed the established order of things. He changed the way we understood a whole list of things from success to happiness, poverty to wealth, humans to God. So forget whatever you might think he stood for and take a look at the facts of his life; we'll look at his words, his death and his resurrection over the next few chapters, but for now let's put his life under the microscope.

The only place in the Bible where we can read about Jesus's life is in the first four books of the New Testament which are known as the Gospels. There's no real debate about the fact that Jesus lived and that he went through the situations as described in Matthew, Mark, Luke and John. There are even plenty of other documents from the time that mention Jesus. I'm happy to assume that these four records of Jesus's life can be trusted.

Having got that out of the way it's time to read them. You might like to do it yourself, perhaps starting with the book of John, but before you do it would be good to make a couple of mental notes. First, C.S. Lewis – whom I mentioned in the first chapter – reckoned that reading the Gospels forces you to come to one of three conclusions. You can choose to believe that Jesus was mad. After all anyone who claims to be God, to be able to forgive sin and raise people from the dead seems to have many of the necessary qualifications to secure a place in a psychiatric ward where the furniture is screwed down and the cutlery is plastic. If you don't go for the crazy Jesus option, Mr Lewis thought that you could choose the bad boy option. If he wasn't mad and if he really did know that he wasn't God, that he couldn't forgive sins and that he couldn't raise people from the dead, then it would seem fair to conclude that Jesus was a

GOD AND THE UNDERDOGS

pretty nasty guy. To deliberately delude and fool
people about such important things is certainly not
the mark of a gentleman. But if mad or bad doesn't
take your fancy, the only option left for you to take is
to believe that he was who he said he was: that Jesus
believed what he said and was able to do what he
offered. It's up to you to decide which one to go for.

But it's not like once you've decided you've got it
all sussed: looking at Jesus's life I am constantly
surprised. Just like any other human he is unpredict-
able and spontaneous, but unlike anyone I've ever
met he continually does the right thing, even when
doing the right thing means doing something new,
unexpected and controversial. He acts with such
integrity that I think it's impossible not to be
impressed.

He was born the son of a carpenter and followed
his dad into the family business. Now in those days
being a chippie wasn't a bad trade at all, it may not
have been the most obvious starting point for a
revolutionary, but it wasn't a bad start. Apart from
his birth and a trip to the synagogue when he was a
boy we don't hear much about him until he hits thirty.
Then things get a little crazy. We follow him over an
intense three and a half year period where he travels
around the country on foot telling people that he is
the Son of God, the Saviour they have all been waiting
for.

Just like any other rabbi, Jesus made sure that he

81

had a collection of people following him whom he could teach and travel with. He picked twelve of them, and these disciples formed an interesting collective. Perhaps you might think that Jesus would have hand-picked a group of stunning individuals who gelled as a team and could be trusted to carry out his requests with the utmost commitment and reliability. You'd be wrong. Jesus picked a group of half-witted rejects and placed the future of the world in their hands. He didn't opt for the most intelligent, most progressive or the most adaptable bunch to be his crew. He chose a bunch of losers.

One of his key players was Peter, a guy who simply found it impossible to keep his mouth shut. He was always talking without thinking and making promises that he couldn't keep. The two of them met one day when Peter was sitting by the Sea of Galilee repairing his nets after a trip out on the lake (don't ask me why they called it a sea, it is most definitely a lake). Jesus was midway through a sermon by the lake when he decided that, having seen Peter's boat, things would be more comfortable if he preached from the boat which was parked on the shore. After he finished preaching Peter returned from washing his nets to find some bloke taking it easy in his vessel. As if that wasn't cheeky enough, when he approached Jesus, he was told to take him out onto the lake for a quick bit of fishing. Peter must have been utterly gobsmacked by Jesus's bottle, as instead of telling him where to go he made do with some seriously heavy sarcasm.

'Master,' he says, 'we have worked hard all night and haven't caught anything. But because you say so I will let down the nets.'

Imagine the scene: Peter, the fisherman being given fishing advice from Jesus, the carpenter. Peter had been hard at it but was in the slightly embarrassing situation of not having caught anything. To be told what to do by someone who was more used to making ashtrays than reading the waters was a bit of a tough one to swallow. 'We have worked hard . . .,' he said, making it clear that he and his two mates were the professionals when it came to fishing. When it came to 'But if you say so . . .' I think it was probably delivered in the kind of tone reserved for humouring small children.

Still, feeling generous Peter took Jesus out on the lake and went through the motions of letting down his nets. Imagine his surprise when by the end of the session they had caught enough fish to fill two boats to sinking point. Not bad for a first timer.

Not only do we read about this time when he had fished all night and come up with nothing, but there's a story later on that seems almost identical; Peter was again empty-handed by the Sea of Galilee after an all-nighter when Jesus (this time having risen from the dead) approaches and tells him to try casting his nets on the other side of the boat. Again he has a result. We suspect that Peter was not the most accomplished of fishermen.

There were another couple of disciples who were brothers, called James and John. They were nick-named Sons of Thunder, not because of their volatile bowel movements but because of their tempers. If there was a fight brewing you could always rely on them to be the ones stirring it.

Then there was Matthew, a tax collector – the profession which might have guaranteed decent money, but also brought with it hatred and suspicion of virtually all his fellow Jews. Thomas earned the name Doubting Thomas because of his complete inability to see anything other than the negative side of things. He was the ultimate pessimist, refusing even to believe that Jesus had risen from the dead in the way that he said he was going to. In fact the only one of the twelve disciples who seemed to have any ingenuity or intelligence, the only one who had any accounting skills was the guy they allowed to look after the purse, Judas Iscariot. He was taking money for himself for ages and wound up handing Jesus over to the Romans to be tried and killed.

It wasn't the case that these were the best he could get, nor was it a project that went wrong. Jesus loved the disciples; he hand-picked them and made sure they were the ones who got to know him far better than any other person around at the time.

Just look at the sort of things that Jesus did. I love

the fact that the first miracle he performed was to turn water into wine at a wedding in Cana. This wasn't a sermon illustration or his part of a deal that meant the guests had to give him their money or attention. It was a disaster; they'd run out of wine – it was a gift, pure and simple. He did it with the sole purpose of letting people have a good time, and he made sure that there was plenty to go round, converting it by the gallon. What's more, the only people who actually knew that the miracle had taken place were the servants, those who were working hard behind the scenes and who weren't soaking up the luxury of the party.

I also love the story of him feeding five thousand people. The preaching had obviously been going down a bomb to have attracted such a large crowd, and when the disciples bring up the subject of food they obviously think it's going to signal the end of the session. They suggest turning people away without even thinking that Jesus may be about to pull a miracle out of the bag. The Bible tells us that Jesus already knew what he was going to do, but that he wanted to test them. He tells his men, 'You feed them,' and we can only assume that they slope off with the worried grumbles of a group of people who are about to end up with a lot of very hungry and very angry people on their backs.

While they're whingeing about how it would take more than eight months' wages to feed them all,

Andrew comes back having been on a search. He's nicked some poor kid's packed lunch and offers Jesus the five loaves and two fish. Jesus takes this tiny amount, blesses it, gives thanks and hands it back to the disciples telling them to do the deed and hand it out to the hungry thousands. The miracle actually happens in the disciples' hands as they hand out what seems to be an almost endless supply of food. This is so key to understanding Jesus: that he doesn't hold onto his power and abilities for himself, but that he gets his people to carry out his work too. That doesn't mean he's lazy, it means that like his Father in heaven, he is mad keen on getting us involved. Christianity is about interaction. It's not a passive trip that we sit back on and enjoy the ride – it's a joint venture. Jesus takes the little that we have, he sees what little we can do and multiplies it until it's enough to impact a multitude.

There was the time (you can read it for yourself in John 4) when travelling through Samaria – the territory of the enemies of the Jews – Jesus stopped by a well having sent his disciples into the town to get provisions. He stays back from the town centre just so that he can meet one particular woman. In the heat of the noonday sun she arrived to get her water. The only people who were mad enough to go out at that time of day were those who weren't allowed out when the day was cooler. This Samaritan was obviously excluded from the rest of polite society, and in the conversation that follows between her and Jesus we understand why.

First he asks her for a drink. Shocked, she reminds him of the stupidity of his suggestion; she is a Samaritan and he is a Jew. In that culture a man didn't initiate a conversation with a woman, and he certainly didn't give the time of day to a Samaritan. He was breaking two rules just so that he could do what happened next. They talk about water and he tells her how he is the living water. They talk about worship and eventually Jesus tells her to go and fetch her husband. She has no husband, she confesses.

'You are right when you say that you have no husband,' says Jesus. 'The fact is you have had five husbands and the man you are with now is not your husband.'

Her reply is the most understated in the whole Bible: 'Sir, I can see you are a prophet.'

Jesus made sure that he met her in the world she lived in every day: an outcast on the edge of society. He spent time with her and showed her the dignity she deserved as a person. She was the wrong sex, the wrong race and the wrong type of person. For this one immoral person Jesus missed out on going into a crowded town full of good Jewish men and women. Eventually she brings along the rest of the towns-people, telling them what had happened to her at the well, and they also believed in him.

Jesus's life has these kinds of patterns in it. He

always went with the servants, the underdogs, the disciples and the outcasts. Through them he reached the rest of society, and the plan remains the same today. If you want to get into Christianity you need to know that it's not some private little religion that just goes on in your room. Christianity, following the Christ, means a whole lot more than tacking a little bit of church onto your normal life. It means going where Jesus goes – to the poor, the broken and the outcast, showing them the love of Jesus and joining his work. There were so many other crazy and wonderful things that he did with his life: put them together and you get a message that only Jesus could have preached.

KEN'S STORY

This follows on from Jeannie's story . . .

I obviously was extremely upset by Joanna's death and did think about the whole question of life, work, family and God. When people said to me that Joanna had gone to heaven I thought he could not have it both ways – to be a God who cared and yet who still allowed Joanna to die and go to heaven.

A few months after Joanna's death I got back into my previous routine of working and not thinking any more about God. When Jeannie started going to church, I thought it was a crutch that she needed and an emotional female response that was not relevant to me. When Jeannie became a Christian and it appeared to me that she was getting more involved with church activities, I started to resent her commitment to the 'church', which seemed more than her commitment to me and the family. As time passed I began to think that Jeannie relied more on God than on me. In the past she had relied on me so much that it definitely felt as if this had changed. I felt that this was coming between us and was even putting our relationship in jeopardy.

It was two and a half years after Joanna died that we went on a winter's holiday in January to Florida for two weeks, which should have been a wonderful time away. However, I was not feeling very happy and seemed to have a lot of anger inside me which I took out on the family. Two weeks after we returned there was a Friday night social with food at St Andrew's Church with a visiting speaker called Canon Keith de Berry. I went along reluctantly – mainly for the food. Some other non-Christian neighbours were also going. After we had eaten Keith spoke about the dangers in a marriage when one partner was a Christian and the other partner wasn't, and the problems this could cause. I felt as if he was speaking directly to me as what he was saying was a reality to me. He then said that if you wanted to find out the answers to these problems, to come along to church on Sunday when he would be speaking. I thought this was a typical church con to get people like me to go to church.

On that Sunday morning Jeannie went to church and I didn't as I am not an early riser! When she came home she said that I should have gone as he spoke so logically, in a way that

I would have appreciated. I said, 'Hard luck, it's too late now.' It was a mild January afternoon and I was doing some gardening. At 6 p.m. I went inside to get changed to go to church. Alex, my eight-year-old daughter said, 'Where are you going?' I replied, 'To church.' She then said, 'No, Daddy, don't be silly. Where are you really going?' I replied, 'Yes, I'm going to church – on my own.'

I did not realise that church got so crowded so early so I crept in and sat at the back. When Keith de Berry spoke he said that for some people their life was like an onion and as you peeled off each layer from the surface you eventually arrived at a centre which is hollow and empty. As I thought about all the material possessions that I had plus my wife and two daughters and friends, I realised that deep inside I was not satisfied and felt hollow and empty. Keith said that the only way to fill that emptiness was to ask Jesus to come into your life and fill you up. He then said it was as easy as the three Rs – Repent, Receive and Rely. I joined in the simple prayer of commitment and asked Jesus into my life as my Lord and Saviour and asked him to fill me up.

I did not particularly feel anything at all but

mentioned to Barry Kissell on leaving the service that I had said the prayer of commitment and he seemed genuinely pleased. When I got home I put my arms around Jeannie and told her what had just happened. She was amazed and didn't believe me at first. For the rest of the evening she said she could not look at me because my face had such a radiance and peace that it was a bit awesome and scary. For the first time since we had been married she couldn't speak to me for the rest of the evening because she couldn't believe what she was seeing and hearing.

The next morning as I was walking from the station to my office there was a cold wind and my head was bowed, but suddenly I thought, NO, I have Jesus in my life and I held my head up high.

Ken Morgan

7

The Radical Words of God

It is impossible to tell the story of Jesus without looking at the things that he said. Like any good teacher of the day Jesus spoke to people and educated them using stories, parables and a big dose of claims so outrageous they shocked a whole nation. To understand some of the scandalous things that he said we need to understand the culture of the day, but many of his claims still have the power to shock today. What his words boiled down to was a brand new way to live, one that challenged all the preconceived ideas about how things should be done. Jesus was a radical, considered so dangerous that they killed him to try and guarantee his silence.

There aren't many better examples of Jesus preaching his message than the lengthy account of his Sermon on the Mount. This was a session when Jesus was on a roll:

'Blessed are you who are poor,
for yours is the kingdom of God.
Blessed are you who hunger now,
for you will be satisfied.
Blessed are you who weep now,
for you will laugh.
Blessed are you when men hate you,
when they exclude you and insult you
and reject your name as evil,
because of the Son of Man.'

(Luke 6:20–2)

The sermon is also recorded in Matthew's telling of
Jesus's story. He follows this bit up with an amazing
reworking of an old law:

'You have heard that it was said, "Eye for eye and
tooth for tooth." But I tell you, Do not resist an
evil person. If someone strikes you on the right
cheek, turn to him the other also. And if someone
wants to sue you and take your tunic, let him have
your cloak as well. If someone forces you to go
one mile, go with him two miles. Give to the one
who asks you and do not turn away from the one
who wants to borrow from you.

'You have heard that it was said, "Love your
neighbour and hate your enemy." But I tell you:
Love your enemies and pray for those who
persecute you, that you may be sons of your Father

94

in heaven. He causes his sun to rise on the evil and the good and sends rain on the righteous and the unrighteous.' (Matthew 5:38–45)

These words have influenced many people throughout time. Mahatma Gandhi, a Hindu, was profoundly affected by Jesus's message of turning the other cheek. These words formed the core of his own message of non-violent resistance that managed to bring an end to British colonial rule in India and Pakistan. Even though I think he failed to understand that there was so much more behind the words of Jesus, he achieved so much.

Then there was that little old Albanian nun who worked in the slums of Calcutta, caring for the dying and the poor who had nowhere else to go. She was a Christian who based her work on the life and words of Jesus. Again, she set an example so powerful that people from world leaders to small children knew that the name of Mother Teresa stood for justice and for the same things that Jesus stood for. Some years ago there was a poll taken among world leaders asking who they thought was the most influential person on the planet. Mother Teresa came out top.

Earlier in history there was an Englishman named William Wilberforce. He was a wealthy MP who played a key role in abolishing slavery not only in the United Kingdom, but also throughout the world. He worked hard to alleviate poverty and was one of the most talked about and respected people of his day. Where did the inspiration come from? Jesus and the words that you've just read above.

The Bible records an incident that happened when Jesus saw some high-ranking religious men lay into a woman who had been caught in adultery (John 8:1–11). They flung her in front of him and tried to trick him asking if she should be stoned there and then. This was the law, and they had it in mind to trap him. What Jesus did was one step ahead. He knelt down and started to write something in the dirt on the ground. We don't know what it was that he wrote – some suggest that it was the secret sins that each of the accusers there was guilty of committing – but after a while he invited whoever thought that they were without sin to step up and take the first shot. No one knows why they did, but one by one the accusers left the scene. Jesus then looked up at the woman who was clearly guilty.

'Woman,' he asked her, 'is there no one left to condemn you?'

'No one, sir,' she replied.

Jesus responded with some amazing words: 'Neither do I condemn you . . . Go and sin no more.' He changed that woman's life for ever; he saved her from death and he saved her from herself. He didn't pretend that what she had been doing wasn't sin, but he revealed to her as he reveals to us the love, mercy and forgiveness of God.

Jesus said things that turned the world on its head. To the people who heard him speak he made it clear that if they acted on his words, they too would play a part in changing the course of history. The offer still stands today.

There are lots of places throughout the Bible that record Jesus claiming to be the Son of God. There's a key passage not long after the incident with the woman caught in adultery. A bunch of Jewish men were arguing with him about whether they were the descendants of Abraham, one of the main figures in the Old Testament. Jesus pulls no punches and has a go at them about disobeying their Father in heaven and they accuse him of being a mixture of demon-possessed and a Samaritan. This calls for Jesus to lay the truth on the line: 'I tell you the truth, if anyone keeps my word, he will never see death' (John 8:51). This makes them all get a tad overexcited and they start falling over themselves to write him off as a nutter. 'Are you greater than our father Abraham? He died, and so did the prophets. Who do you think you are?' I wonder if one day they realised the outrageousness of their question. I mean, who did they think *they* were to ask it?

Jesus replied, 'If I glorify myself, my glory means nothing. My father, whom you claim as your God, is the one who glorifies me. Though you do not

know him, I know him. If I said I did not, I would
be a liar like you, but I do know him and keep his
word. Your father Abraham rejoiced at the thought
of seeing my day; he saw it and was glad.'

'You are not yet fifty years old,' the Jews said to
him, 'and you have seen Abraham!'

'I tell you the truth,' Jesus answered, 'before
Abraham was born, I am.' At this, they picked up
stones to stone him, but Jesus hid himself, slipping
away from the temple grounds. (John 8:54–9)

This passage is massively significant, even though it
is a little confusing. We understand that Jesus died
and rose again, that he was God, but all that stuff
about 'I am' can easily go right over our heads. It
must have been significant though, just look again at
their reaction.

The whole 'I am' thing has its roots way back in
the forming of the nation of Israel. God had called
Moses out to a place in the desert where he spoke
through a burning bush, telling Moses that he was
the one who was going to lead his people out of the
slavery of Egypt. Cleverly asking for some ID, Moses
asked the bush/God who he should tell the people
had sent him on such a bold mission.

'Say "I am" has sent you,' came the reply.

'I am' is a name for God, and, as any good Jew
would know, when Jesus said that he was 'I am',
he was claiming to be God himself.

Later there's an interesting bit of stuff going on in John chapter 20 when Jesus has risen from the dead. As usual it's Thomas who is having a hard time believing the truth behind what's going on, mainly because he is the only one of the disciples who is yet to see the risen Jesus. He knows himself too well to be able to take their word for it, and he tells them that unless he sees the nail marks and the hole in his side, he will not believe that the person the others claim to have seen really is Jesus himself.

Just then, guess what happens? Jesus appears. Not through the door mind you – the disciples knew that it was well and truly bolted for fear of further attacks by the Romans – or through the wall, proper ghost style. He just appears, walks up to Thomas and says to him,

'Put your finger here, see my hands. Reach out your hand and put it into my side. Stop doubting and believe.'
    Thomas said to him, 'My Lord and my God.'
    Then Jesus told him, 'Because you have seen me, you have believed; blessed are those who have not seen me and yet have believed.' (John 20:27–9)

When Thomas saw and called Jesus his God, Jesus didn't rebuke him. Instead he accepted Thomas's declaration that he was God. In a way many of us can sympathise with Tom: there's so much hype around these days that it can be useful for us not to believe everything we see and hear. After all, he was only being cautious, wouldn't you be? There is a difference though between now and then, and Jesus's words picked up on it. Tom was one of the last to see him in the flesh, as from then on he was back in heaven, allowing his Holy Spirit to carry out the work here on earth. Tom was used to seeing God in physical form, but now we have to rely on seeing him in other ways. We can read the Bible and we can ask God, by his Spirit, to make himself known to us. We can pray and listen to what he says. We can take time to meditate on the things that reveal his character, like creation, human people and the Bible. The point is that we have to make a choice either to believe without seeing God in the flesh or not to believe at all. How could Jesus do this? Was this a mistake, the result of him getting bored or cutting corners? No. Jesus had completed his work and had made sure that future believers would have enough to go on, enough to believe that he was exactly who he said he was. Jesus's words were dynamite. They changed everything from how we see the poor, to how we see death, to how we see ourselves. They show us that he was God and they make it clear that we have to grab hold of what he has said for ourselves. Read the Bible and ask God for help; you might not be able to put your fingers in his wounds but you sure can find out what's in his heart.

TARYN'S STORY

At the age of two I caught measles, despite having a jab. I didn't recover and after tests I was diagnosed as having Nephritic Syndrome – a kidney disease. This was the beginning of many long stays in hospital. During this time I became increasingly poorly. It was explained to my family that there were three responses to the steroids I was on: steroid responsive, steroid dependent or steroid resistant. I had started off responsive, became dependent and then eventually became resistant. We were warned that unless there was a dramatic change, I would be moved to Great Ormond Street Hospital to try a toxic drug regime. This would have permanent and damaging side-effects.

A prayer chain was immediately set up, with all the Christians we knew (and many we didn't) praying for me. During this time God used a verse in the Bible to speak to us. It came from Psalm 46 (in the King James Version): 'God is in the midst of her; she shall not be moved: God shall help her, and that right early.' This was a promise that God was going to help me, and sure enough there was a dramatic improvement! The doctors were amazed and baffled. That day there was much rejoicing and giving thanks to the Lord for his continuing faithfulness to us.

At around the same time, we moved from Essex to Devon and I was transferred to a hospital in Exeter. I was referred to a specialist at Bristol because the doctors were concerned about my repeated relapses. They wanted to do a renal biopsy with all its related risks. We were given an early morning appointment in Bristol and whilst my parents were contemplating a very early morning start, a Christian doctor spotted a Bible on my locker. He had heard that we hadn't been in the area long and offered us lodgings at his sister's house in Bristol for the night – God's provision again!

Before we went, the Lord gave us another promise: 'You will go out in joy and be led forth in peace' (Isaiah 55:12). Throughout the next day we clung on to these words to try and banish the fears that we were all feeling.

The specialist told us what we had been longing to hear, that he was sure I would grow out of this illness given time. (We had learnt by this stage that the medical profession do not raise false hopes and always point out the worst scenario.) It was another promise from God that he was looking after me. There were many tears of happiness that day and I remember skipping with my mum and dad down the street. We were so happy! God had given us so much joy.

I was baptised at the age of seven. I had no doubt about my faith nor about my reasons for being baptised. I wanted to show everyone that I loved Jesus and wanted to do his will for the rest of my life.

Over the years my relapses became less frequent. I was discharged from hospital at the age of twelve. On my final visit my doctor called in some junior and student doctors to see me. He told them, 'Next time you see a little one very poorly, remember Taryn, she has been there and look at her now!' I had no doubt in my mind that the Lord had made me well again.

From the age of twelve to fifteen I was completely healthy. I relapsed during Christmas 1993 and became very ill again. It was a very painful time for my family and me. I put on about four stone in weight and puffed up like a balloon. I felt like a complete freak and contemplated suicide twice, but something was holding me back and I knew that something was God. Even during the darkest days I knew that I wasn't alone. Slowly but surely the Lord began to soften my heart and really challenged me. He showed me time and time again that if I only trusted in him, he would never let me down. That wasn't to say that there wouldn't be hard times but I had learnt that even in the most despairing hour he can turn things around for the better. Here I am now, five years on, completely well and feeling great!

Taryn Bibby

8

God and the Ultimate Sacrifice

I once saw a calf being born. I was about ten years old and was excited enough at the fact that I had been allowed to stay up till such a late hour, let alone seeing a cute-looking baby calf take its first stumbling steps in the world. The Pilavachis were staying on a farm in Devon, and the farmer had been talking excitedly ever since we arrived about his prized heifer and her impending labour. I'll never forget the sense of wonder as he calmed the mother down. The anxious excitement as those spindly legs first appeared and the sheer joy of seeing that everything was all right. My dad and I watched intently, and as the mother licked the calf down I plucked up the courage to break the silence. I asked what he would call the new baby.

'Oh, it'll not need a name,' he replied. 'This one will be hamburger by the time it's two.'

It took me weeks to recover. The thought that

something could be born just so that it could die sent me into a deep well of confusion. That was probably what started me writing bad poetry, and to be honest I still have trouble forcing down the second double cheeseburger.

At the risk of being irreverent, there is a similarity between a calf born for the table and the Son of God who was born for our sins. Now that all sounds quite nice and pain free, no? I mean 'born for our sins' doesn't exactly send a shiver down your spine – it's preferable to 'dying for our sins' any day of the week. Hold on, though, 'cos the truth is out there. For Jesus, being born for our sins meant paying for our sins. The truth about sin is that it demanded a big payment. The Jews had been paying theirs off in instalments for hundreds of years. Take a look at the first few books of the Bible and you'll see how they were told by God to stick to the rules (you can read them for yourself in Exodus 20 – there are ten of them). When they messed up the deal was that they would pass their sin on to a goat or a pure and perfect lamb offered as a sacrifice to the Lord. These sacrifices all pointed towards the ultimate sacrifice that one day would come and replace their rituals: the perfect and blemish free lamb that would pay for them all.

Throughout the Old Testament this role of Jesus is hidden, but by the time we reach the New he is revealed. As John the Baptist sees him for the first time he cries out, 'Behold, the Lamb of God . . .' He immediately recognised not only who Jesus was, but why he was here. God sent his own Son down to earth so that he could pay the debt of all our sin. This wasn't going to be easy as what was owing wasn't just the sins of the Israelites, but all the rest of the people in the world too. What's more he didn't just stick to the present day, Jesus paid for all the sins that people would commit in the future as well. In terms of doves, sheep and cows that adds up to . . . Well, it actually adds up to far more than can ever be counted. Jesus died once and for all so that we might escape God's judgment.

Jesus's blood had to be shed. In the last chapter we mentioned Moses who was sent by God to bring freedom to his people. It was a struggle and God had to send loads of plagues and stuff to make the Egyptians that were holding his people captive let them go. The last plague was when God passed over Egypt and killed the first-born son of each Egyptian family. When he did that he told the Israelites to slaughter a lamb beforehand and smear its blood over the doorway of their house so that God would pass over their home and spare their lives. When Jesus died as the ultimate sacrificial lamb, his blood appears on us and we too escape the punishment of God.

The cross is central to Christianity. It may have been just two bits of wood, but Christians believe that when Jesus died on one it changed world history. There were other people who were crucified; criminals, traitors and revolutionaries. It was a particularly barbaric way to kill someone, blending agonising pain with long term exhaustion and an inevitable crawl towards an undignified end. It was to the Romans what a gas chamber was to the Nazis and what the electric chair is to America. It was reserved for the very worst of criminals, but it ended up killing the very best of men.

Understanding that Jesus was born to die is not like saying that Ryan Giggs was born to score *that goal* against Arsenal or that I was born to eat. Jesus was born for something so miraculous yet so costly that his whole life was a build-up to one simple act of barbaric cruelty. He was treated as a common criminal, was mis-tried, falsely accused and left to die, all because the Roman authorities wanted an easy life and the Jewish religious leaders felt threatened by him.

In the book of Romans it says that the pay-back from sin is death. In other words, living away from the source of all life can only lead by itself to one conclusion: separation from God. Just like any other crime, the offence that we humans committed first of all in turning away from God demanded some kind of payment if we are ever to approach God. He is so holy and perfect that he simply cannot look on sin. At the same time the love and mercy of God could not bear to look away from his creations.

Of all the torture that he went through when he was crucified – of the nails in his hands and feet, the spear in his side and the slow suffocation as his exhaustion made it harder to breathe – I am sure that the worst thing he went through was that for a period of time Jesus was separated from his Father. For the first and only time in all eternity Jesus was alone, crying out at one point, 'My God, my God, why have you forsaken me?' That must have been the worst punishment imaginable for the Son of God. At that moment the sins of all the world were heaped upon him as he bore the punishment for all the things we have done wrong. Taking all our dirt, shame and pain on himself meant that God the Father had to look away, and, if we define hell as 'being totally without God', then for those moments the Son of God was in hell.

In dying Jesus managed to put right all that we had put wrong. When we chose to live apart from God, following our own selfish desires instead of his will, a barrier got erected between us and him. It became impossible for us to break through and reach God but Jesus's death managed to reunite us with him.

Jesus was the ultimate sacrificial lamb, the sacrifice that no human could give. Because he was such a perfect and precious substitute we no longer have to pay a price, all we have to do is ask God to have mercy on us. We know that the punishment we really deserve is death – living away from him and serving our own selfish desires can ultimately lead to nothing else – but we can ask God not to look at our sin, but to remember the cross and all that Jesus did for us, and ask him to have mercy. Through what Jesus did we can again return to having a relationship with God our Father, we can again be adopted by him.

Think of it as being like a shopping trip, one with a full trolley at the end. You approach the till, have your goods swiped and get asked how you intend to pay for what you've loaded up. With Jesus next to you he pipes up 'I'll pay', and promptly gets in the till himself, allowing us to move on.

But to look at the cross without looking at what happened next is like trying to understand quantum physics without a calculator or like trying to sell a diet product by only using the 'before' picture instead of the skinny 'after' shot as well. The cross and the resurrection cannot be separated because they were the final goal of Jesus's time on earth. If there was no resurrection, if Jesus had stayed dead, then Christianity would be nothing more than a collection of decent ideas on how to treat people. Perhaps it might have caught on in the way that odd fashions do, but it would never have had the power needed to keep people going. The truth, on the other hand, is that Jesus did rise from the dead, he did come back to life, so Christianity does have power. Jesus's words and everything he stood for and promised were true.

The fact that Jesus had told them that he would rise again did not stop the disciples from thinking that it was all over once Jesus had been buried. The fact that the Scriptures described what would happen next was not much in the way of comfort, and when we join them at the end of each of the Gospels, we get a clear picture of just how depressed they are. It doesn't stay that way for long though, and looking at their intense reactions when they see Jesus alive and in the flesh after his death teaches us some important lessons.

Mary Magdalene – the prostitute whom Jesus had cared for, respected and treated with dignity – was on her way to look after Jesus's body in the tomb. Having gone back to tell the disciples she returned and stood weeping outside the place where Jesus had been laid to rest.

As she wept, she bent over to look into the tomb and saw two angels in white, seated where Jesus' body had been, one at the head and the other at the foot.

They asked her, 'Woman, why are you crying?'

'They have taken my Lord away,' she said, 'and I don't know where they have put him.' At this, she turned round and saw Jesus standing there, but she did not realise that it was Jesus.

Mary's grief was so intense that she couldn't even recognise the most important man in her life. She had spent time with him, learnt from him and been saved by him yet she couldn't tell him apart from a stranger.

What Jesus said next is interesting. I'm sure that he knew why she was crying but still he asked. Perhaps he wanted her to admit her fears.

> 'Woman,' he said, 'why are you crying? Who is it you are looking for?'
> Thinking he was the gardener, she said, 'Sir, if you have carried him away, tell me where you have put him, and I will get him.'

Perhaps he was having a laugh, as the situation soon descends into a farce with Mary thinking that he has come to trim the hedges. It only took one word to put her straight:

> Jesus said to her, 'Mary.'
> She turned towards him and cried out in Aramaic, 'Rabboni!' (which means Teacher). (John 20:11–16)

All that Jesus had to do was say her name, probably in the same way that he had always said it. That was enough for her to know exactly who he was.

Later we read about the wonderful time when

Jesus appeared to Thomas. We've already had a quick look, but remember how much of a sceptic Thomas was, how he never believed anything at first? When Jesus showed up and told Thomas to feel his wounds it was exactly the right thing to do. In just the same way that speaking Mary's name allowed her to realise who he was, so letting Thomas see the evidence was enough to allow him to see the truth. 'My Lord and my God!' he said (John 20:28), suddenly aware that Jesus was exactly who he said he was. A ghost wouldn't have been able to convince Thomas: it had to be the real thing, which is exactly what he got. Believe me, this is how it can be with us: one moment of contact when Jesus calls us by name or shows himself to us can be enough to change the way we see him forever.

There were many other people who saw Jesus in the six weeks that he spent on earth after he had been crucified, buried and had risen from the dead, but his resurrection didn't just affect them. Because he rose from the dead Jesus put power into the faith. Because of his own power over death we too are no longer slaves to death or sin; we can also enjoy life after death with God when we die as well as new life here on earth as we enjoy a living relationship with Jesus. Through his death Jesus not only took the punishment for all our sin, he also made it possible for Christians to say 'I know Jesus'. He isn't just a historical figure or a good but dead man, he is around today and available for his people to reach him. Death couldn't beat him, hell couldn't keep him but you and I can meet him.

PAULINE'S STORY

From an early age I showed great promise, both at school and in music. It was no hardship to me to read and study and I suppose I could have accurately been described as a bit of a swot! There were some (including myself at the time) who felt I had everything going for me. Life seemed pretty set and a first class degree from Cambridge was on the horizon.

In my mid-teens I realised that underneath the seemingly competent high-achiever was someone who was distinctly unhappy with herself and with life. I found that my intense pursuit of achievement had left me lonely, unable to relate well to people of my own age; and despite having so much success, I felt inferior to my friends, desperately wanting to be part of the crowd but always feeling 'less than': less fun, less attractive, less popular, less wanted.

Coupled with this, many questions about life were raised when a school friend was tragically killed in a car accident. What is it all about? Where are we going? Who am I? Why am I so empty?

About this time I took a holiday job which

was quite physically exerting and without trying I began to lose some weight. As people commented on how good I looked I began to feel a bit more in control. With a bit of effort I could have the figure I wanted, feel less inferior to my friends and, more to the point, feel happier with myself.

Unfortunately I didn't stop there. As I began to lose weight I started to feel a 'high' at having such a control over my body. It was as if another world had begun, full of weight loss plans, exercise plans and calorie counting. My whole mind was obsessed with food and weight. What had begun as a series of choices was fast becoming a life-controlling addiction. I began to feel as if I was the slave of a cruel master, unable to stop the self-destruction that I had begun. I was out of control and unable to let anyone to help me. Part of me didn't even want to be helped – what did life have to offer anyway? I began to admit that I had a serious problem, that I was in fact anorexic.

At the end of my first year at Cambridge I was admitted to the eating disorders unit of a London hospital at five stone. Not only did I have no body left, my mind, feelings and personality were dead too. I had no will to live.

I didn't feel that there was anyone left inside. Through the hospital programme I gained four stone over nine months and was discharged with everyone hoping that things were 'all better now'. But nothing inside had changed. There was no hope or desire in me for life, and six months later I was five stone again and being readmitted to hospital for another nine months. The terror of having to eat in hospital was intense and my world remained dominated with fear and food obsession.

A further nine months of treatment ensued, again I left hospital four stone heavier, and again I lost it all over the next six months. By that time a friend of mine mentioned that it would be good for me to talk to a friend of hers from a prayer group. Not particularly keen on the idea but with nothing to lose I met her and told how I was feeling. Over the next few weeks and months she continued to meet me and began to talk about knowing God. I had always believed in God and even prayed as a young girl, but she was talking about knowing him in a different way. Slowly I began to wonder, would he help me? It seemed that no one else could.

I left hospital for the third time and began attending the prayer group. I loved being there but felt out of it somehow. I watched people as they sang to God and knew that they talked to him and knew him as I didn't. It wasn't long before the old self-destruct feelings and desire to starve came raging up again. I could feel myself losing weight and couldn't bear the thought of going back into hospital, of life being nothing more than this until I died.

One morning, when I thought I could stand no more, I dropped to the floor and cried out to God, 'If you're there, you MUST show me, I'm not leaving this room until I know you exist.' I knew there was nowhere else to turn. Suddenly in the midst of the turmoil and pain it seemed that an intense light, warmth and love broke through on my inside. I could feel him around me and in me and I knew that Jesus was alive. That there in my room, he loved me and accepted me as I came to him, as I was, in all my mess and pain and fear. That he loved me completely and utterly. I was overwhelmed with joy, laughter and tears. 'JESUS IS ALIVE, JESUS IS ALIVE' was all that I could get out of my mouth.

That was the beginning of healing and of real life. Much freedom came in a moment, much more was worked out subsequently. Within four months I was nine stone and, to the amazement of the hospital, never went below that again. More significantly, I knew there was and is a hope. That it is his love and life that changes us, whatever desperate place we are in – thank you, Lord.

Pauline Kirke

9

God in Me

I was sitting in someone's front room just off the Uxbridge Road with my eyes shut tight and my heart beating faster than I thought was probably good for me. Two friends from the church were sat either side, praying in the soft and mellow tones of voice that I had heard Christians use before when they were trying to convince God to do something great. I sneaked a look out of one eye at the clock I had carefully positioned myself opposite. I had been there for two and three-quarter minutes but it felt like years. I tried again to relax.

'Just let God in, Mike,' soothed one of my praying friends.

I tried. I pictured myself opening the doors of my heart to allow his presence to enter gracefully. Nothing. I imagined inviting him in with tea and biscuits and the promise of some telly after we were done. Nothing. I visualised offering him money and a chance to borrow my Simon and Garfunkel records if he would just come in. Still nothing.

Things went on like this for many more minutes. I was supposed to be meeting the Holy Spirit, allowing him to come into my life and do whatever it was he was going to do. I wasn't quite sure what was going to happen, but I was darn sure that it was supposed to be better than this. It was like being constipated only with a chronic case of diarrhoea building up. Why wasn't it working?

My friends carried on praying throughout, thanking God, asking him to meet with me and managing to sound calm and relaxed throughout it all. I was just about to call a halt to it all when I started to feel dizzy. That usually meant that I was hungry, so I decided to keep going. After all, if I broke it off now and disappeared into the kitchen straight away to scoff down a couple of slices of Arctic Roll what would they think of me? I didn't think it was funny, but I started to smile. Pretty soon I felt as though I had drunk the warmest and sweetest drink in the world; I felt a deep happiness and something that I could only describe as joy. I thought it best that I confess and was just about to own up to being an Arctic Roll addict when they both started to clap and thank God for sending me his Spirit.

'That's it, Mike,' one said.

'That's it?' I asked. I was confused for a second but it was soon washed away as I realised that it wasn't my taste buds but it was God who was making me feel great.

Looking back now I'm not surprised that I was confused. Thinking of God as a holy Trinity is hard enough, but breaking it down into the three persons or characteristics of God can be even more of a head-do. OK, so most of us can come up with some kind of idea about what God the Father might be like: we might go with an image or feeling drawn from our ideas of what a perfect father should be like. Thinking of God the Son also tends not to present too many problems as we are all familiar with the form that Jesus took on when he came to earth. Think about God the Spirit though, and we're out of our depth. Do we think of him as some kind of good ghost? A kind force?

The first thing to realise is that the Holy Spirit is not an 'it', he's a 'he'. The Holy Spirit has personality and character just in the same way that the Father and the Son do. We need to know that the Holy Spirit wasn't just called up for action once Jesus returned to heaven: the truth is that he has been part of things since the beginning. Imagine creation: if God the Father had the idea, the Son then spoke the idea into existence and it was the power of the Holy Spirit that brooded over the waters and made it all take shape. The Holy Spirit is the power of God; he is 'God with us' and 'God in us'. When the Bible was translated into one regional dialect in China and they could find no word for spirit or ghost, the translator settled on the phrase 'resident boss'. Someone else once called him 'the go-between God', and both of these can help us understand who he is.

The Holy Spirit is the ultimate in humility. He doesn't exist to make himself known or to raise his own public profile, instead he exists to reveal Jesus to us. The relationship that we can have with him is there simply so that he can teach us more about Jesus, more about who he was, what he did and how we can follow his example. In this way he reveals truth to us, showing the depth of the Scriptures and helping us to apply them to our own lives.

Remember what we were saying in the last chapter about how through Jesus's death we can approach God again? Well it's only possible to do that through the Spirit. Here's the proof:

> For you did not receive a spirit that makes you a slave again to fear, but you received the Spirit of sonship. And by him we cry, 'Abba, Father.'
>
> (Romans 8:15)

Don't get bogged down with images of 1970s' Swedes in glitter. *Abba* means 'Daddy'. So through the Holy Spirit we can have a relationship with God that is truly personal and intimate. We don't deserve it, but like small children we can approach him and sit at his feet, all because the Holy Spirit lives in us and draws us back to him.

But how do you get him? Do you catch, snare or win him? Is it a case of needing to earn enough points before we can collect or do some people get better versions of him than others through being good? The answer is that we receive the Holy Spirit when we become Christians. Without him on board it is impossible to know Jesus and say that he is Lord. To want to know God, to feel that you have enough of a vague idea about what he is like to ask him into your life means that the Holy Spirit has already been working in you, revealing Jesus to you. Things don't just end there though, as once we've become Christians we need to be continually refilled. We all fall far short of the standard set by Jesus so it makes sense that we all need to be given regular help to become more like him.

We also need help to be bold and carry out the job of telling others about Jesus. There are loads of verses in the Bible that back this up, and reading them it seems that one of his favourite things is to inspire us to get out and do the business of spreading the word ourselves.

In John we read Jesus's words:

But the Counsellor, the Holy Spirit, whom the Father will send in my name, will teach you all things, and will remind you of everything I have said to you.

(John 14:26)

And later we find out that the early Church are in on the act too:

> All of them were filled with the Holy Spirit and began to speak in other tongues, as the Spirit enabled them. (Acts 2:4)

And finally:

> This is what we speak, not in words taught us by human wisdom but in words taught by the Spirit, expressing spiritual truths in spiritual words.
>
> (I Corinthians 2:13)

This power that the early Christians received from the Holy Spirit wasn't just able to inspire them to speak, but it also helped them to be Jesus's witnesses (see Acts 1:8), to get out and do the same things that Jesus did. Reading through the rest of the New Testament we can see that the Holy Spirit gave the first Christians a power that they previously didn't have. We can be sure of this because we saw how useless some of them were when they were following Jesus around as his disciples.

The story about me at the beginning of this chapter happened when I had been a Christian for only a few months. I don't know how, but I knew that I needed to have more of the Holy Spirit inside of me. Looking back now I can see that it was a natural desire, but at the time it was all so hard to pin down. My friends prayed that the Holy Spirit would come and fill me up and after a while I just knew that he had. I felt like I was full up on God's love, inspired and passionate, ready to get on with being the most radical Christian that I could. I knew Jesus and loved him already, but something about that afternoon made it clear that by some miracle God wasn't just in heaven, he was actually living within me too. After that time prayer became so much easier and I felt like what I was saying was really getting through, as well as that I was able to listen to what I thought God was saying. It made sense and seemed to be in line with a verse written to the early Church in Rome:

In the same way the Spirit helps us in our weakness. We do not know what we ought to pray for but the Spirit himself intercedes for us with groans that words cannot express. And he who searches our hearts knows the mind of the Spirit, because the Spirit intercedes for the saints in accordance with God's will.
(Romans 8:26)

The Holy Spirit actually helps us to pray, joining up with our spirit and helping us to pray to God the Father and God the Son.

If you want to be filled with God's Spirit, the thing to do is to ask. Jesus said to his disciples that if they thought that good parents knew how to give decent gifts to their children, they should check out just how much more the Father in heaven would give the ultimate good gift of the Holy Spirit to those who asked him. We need to ask, and keep on asking and keep on receiving. I know I tend to leak a little bit, so I'm constantly in need of more of him in my life. If we don't do this then we are relying on our own strength to live the Christian life, and that never works.

As you've been reading this book you've heard about some of the different parts that go to make up this mind-blowing phenomenon called Christianity. It changes lives and turns the world upside down. It can be tough sometimes but there's one final thing to note. It's called joy. Jesus didn't die on the cross just so that we could struggle on our own and God didn't just give us a bag-full of commands to make us feel bad. He gave us power so that it wouldn't be a life of frustration, but one fully furnished with all the fullness that comes from God above. We like to think that we know how to live our own lives: take it from God, he's the ultimate Creator of all life and he knows exactly how to get the most out of it.

Closing Prayer...

So, where do we go from here? If you're not sure about the stuff I've said can I ask that you genuinely investigate further? Find people who say that they know this Jesus and look at their lives to see if there's any evidence there for Jesus. Why not examine the Bible for yourself, read the stories in one of the Gospels and see if it makes sense? It may be that you're ready to get to know this Jesus and to be one of his family. If you are it could be helpful for you to say this simple prayer although you can actually use any form of words you want . . .

Dear Jesus,
I thank you that you died on a cross for me. I want the story of my life to be part of your story. I want to be your follower. Would you forgive me for the things I've thought, said and done that have been selfish and have taken me away from you? Jesus,

come into my life now; fill me with your Holy Spirit and make me a child of your Father. Help me to become more like you and for the time I'm on this earth to serve you by showing your love to your world.

Amen.

So that's it then. If you have said this prayer you have not reached the end of a journey but the beginning. It's the same journey my friends and I are on, of going deeper into God and also out to the world he loves. Welcome to the family.